Following Directions

Name _____

 ## Compose a Name!

Follow the directions to learn the name of a composer.

Start with a word that is used to light a fire. _____

Add a word that means a short rest. _____

Drop the word that means an adult male. _____

Add a word that is a form of precipitation. _____

Add a word that could mean the smallest living thing in your body or a small "room" in a jail. _____

Drop the word that describes the step of a high-stepping horse. _____

Add a word that names a bird that "coos." _____

Drop the double consonant. _____

Drop the fourth letter of the alphabet. Replace it with the eleventh letter. _____

Add the word that contains the sun, stars, etc. _____

Drop the fourth vowel in this word and you will have the last name of this composer. _____

Now learn the name of a ballet he wrote (two words).

Write the name of a prickly plant. (It begins with **th**.) _____

Add the word neat.
Drop the word that means skinny. _____

Add the name of an evergreen tree that begins with p. _____

Drop the two consonants that are the same. _____

Replace the final letter of the word with the seventh letter of the alphabet. _____

Drop the first letter of the alphabet. _____

Add the word that can mean whip or win. _____

Add a word that means to destroy or demolish. _____

Drop the word for a kind of can. _____

Add the name of a spinning toy. _____

Add a word that is the opposite of no. _____

Drop the plural word for something used to tie with. _____

Write the name of the ballet. _____

Following Directions

Stomp Man

Make a dot (•) for each of the following points in order. Connect each point as you make it with the previous one.

1. B,4	6. L,18	11. Q,16	16. V,20	21. U,13	26. W,10	31. T,6	36. R,10
2. B,8	7. M,20	12. O,12	17. U,21	22. Y,12	27. U,8	32. U,7	37. M,10
3. H,8	8. O,21	13. R,12	18. S,16	23. Y,11	28. U,10	33. U,4	38. H,6
4. K,11	9. O,19	14. R,16	19. T,11	24. X,11	29. T,10	34. T,5	39. C,7
5. O,16	10. M,18	15. V,24	20. U,11	25. X,10	30. Q,7	35. P,7	40. B,4

Write a set of points (pairs of numbers) that will show what "Stomp Man" is about to crush. Give your set of points to a classmate to solve. ——→

SET OF POINTS

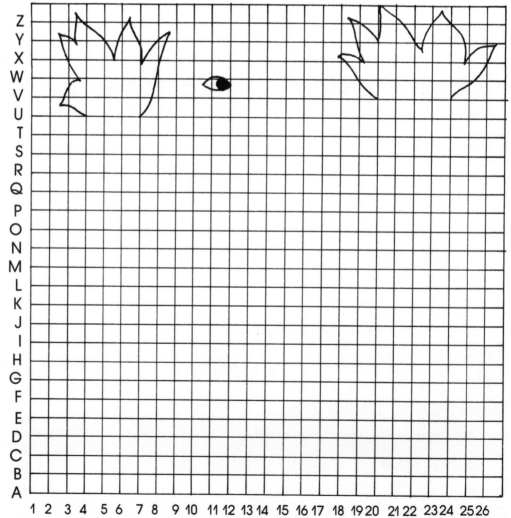

Following Directions

Name _____

Whose House?

Draw as you are directed.

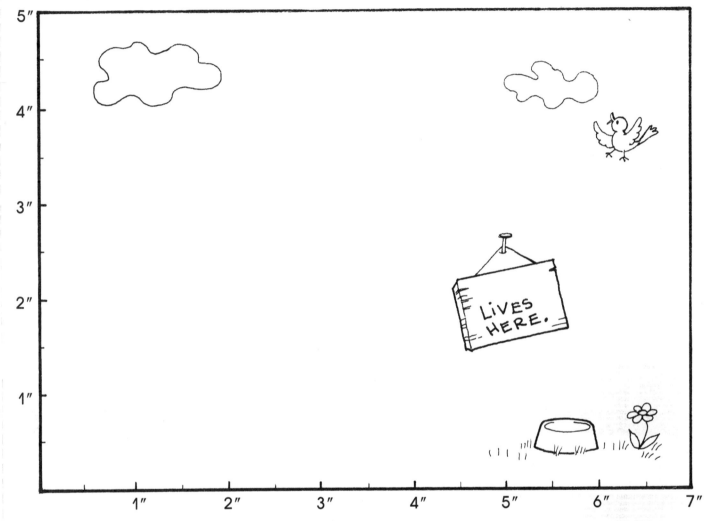

Draw a five inch horizontal line one inch above the base line. Begin the line one inch in from the left.

Draw another five inch horizontal line parallel to the line you just drew, but two inches above it.

Draw a two inch vertical line connecting the left side ends of the two horizontal lines. Draw a two inch vertical line connecting the right side ends of the two horizontal lines.

Make a dot four-and-a-half inches above the base line and three-and-a-half inches from the left side.

Draw a line from the left end of the top horizontal line that you drew to the dot.

Draw a line from the right end of the top horizontal line that you drew to the dot.

Draw a one inch horizontal line two-and-one-half inches above the base line. Begin the line three inches from the left.

Draw two vertical lines—one from the left side and one from the right of the horizontal line you just drew. Make each one go down one-and-a-half inches.

Write who lives here. Fill in the sign and color all of the picture.

Following Directions

Information, Please

When you finish this page, take it home. Keep it in a handy place.

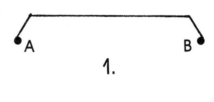

A   B

1.

_____

Part One

Write your family name on line 1.

Write your address on line 2.

Write your phone number on line 3.

Write the name and phone number of a friend on line 4.

Write the name and number of your doctor or medical service on line 5.

Write the emergency number for the area where you live on line 6.

E   C   D   F

5.   2.   6.

_____   _____   _____

Y   _____   _____   Z

_____

I   G   H   J

Part Two

3.

Use a ruler.
Draw a line from:

A to B
A to C
B to D
E to C
D to F
I to G
H to J
G to M and
H to N

Draw a dotted line from:

C to D
C to G
D to H
G to H
K to L
F to J
M to N and E to I

_____

K   L

4.

Part Three

Cut out the figure on the solid lines.

Fold with the written information outward, on the dotted lines.

Put paste on **X**. Tuck flap **X** under **A–B**. Pinch to hold.

Put paste on **Y**. Tuck flap **Y** under **K–M**. Press until it holds.

Put paste on **Z**. Tuck flap **Z** under **L–N**. Press until it holds.

_____

_____

M   X   N

Following Directions

Name _____

Alpha Trail

There are many paths through Alpha Park. Every letter you pass equals points. The object is to get through with as few points as possible. The points are as follows:

Add one for every **M** you pass.
Add two for every **F**.
Add three for every **R**.
Subtract one for every **V**.
Subtract two for every **N**.

Can you find your way through the park under five? Try it.

Following Directions

Name _____

Head Over Heels

There are twelve words in this puzzle. Each word starts from the center box and then follows its own path. Find each one by column and/or row number plus its direction. The first one is done as an example.

Example: 1. The first letter, **4E**, is 4 spaces to the right (East) of the center box.
4E is **C**.
The next letter, **2N**, is 2 spaces above (North) C. **2N** is **H**.
The third letter, **5W**, is 5 spaces to the left (West) of H. **5W** is **E**.
The fourth letter, **3S**, is 3 rows below (South) E. **3S** is an **S**.
The last letter, **2W**, is 2 columns to the left (West) of S. **2W** is **T**.

Begin the next word from the center and follow its pattern. All the letters will be used and they will only be used once. Cross out each letter as it is used.

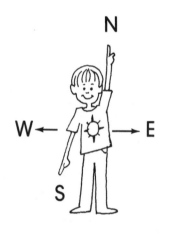

N
W ← → E
S

I	D	S	H	S	R	D	S	E	R	E
N	L	E	G	E	C	A	E	H	H	M
N	V	H	E	I	S	L	G	R	E	O
E	A	L	A	F		T	H	A	C	F
S	S	T	I	S	S	H	S	E	L	P
E	N	B	A	O	W	S	W	S	D	R
T	B	O	S	I	D	U	N	N	K	O

1. **CHEST**
4E, 2N, 5W, 3S, 2W

2. _____
1N, 3W, 4S, 4E, 4N, 2N, 4E, 5S, 4W

3. _____
1W, 3S, 3E, 4N, 2E, 2N, 2W

4. _____
4W, 3S, 4E, 5E, 5N, 3W, 7W

5. _____
5E, 1N, 2W, 2N, 5W, 2S, 3S, 6E

6. _____
2S, 5N, 5W, 4S, 2S, 3E

7. _____
1E, 1S, 3W, 3N, 5E, 4S

8. _____
5W, 2E, 2S, 2E, 3E, 1N

9. _____
3E, 3S, 1E, 2N, 1W, 7W

10. _____
1S, 5E, 2N + 6W, 4W, 3S

11. _____
2E, 4W, 2W + 2S, 5N, 3E

12. _____
2N, 1E, 5W, 1S, 1N + 1E, 1N

IF8712 Reading Skills

Find Your Way

Mary has invited some friends to visit her. Follow her written directions and draw the path her friends should take.

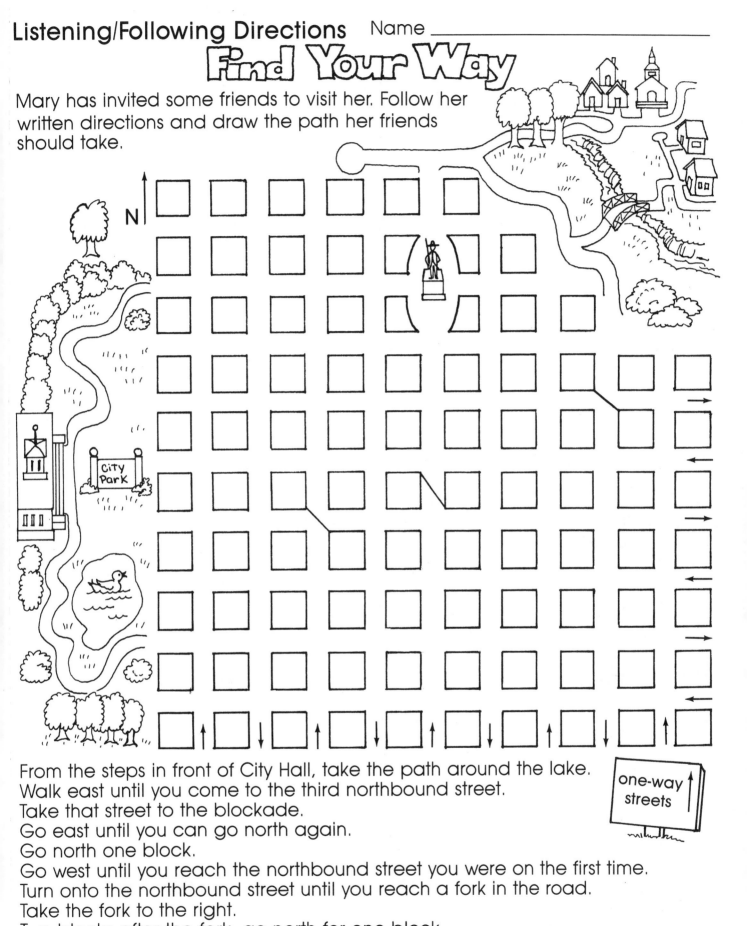

From the steps in front of City Hall, take the path around the lake.
Walk east until you come to the third northbound street.
Take that street to the blockade.
Go east until you can go north again.
Go north one block.
Go west until you reach the northbound street you were on the first time.
Turn onto the northbound street until you reach a fork in the road.
Take the fork to the right.
Two blocks after the fork, go north for one block.
There the path goes through the woods to Mary's house. Mary's house is the
    second one on the left of the church. Circle Mary's house.

one-way streets

2·4·6·8 Who Do We Appreciate?

Use the following number sequence as directed.

2, 4, 6, 8, 10, 12, 14, 16, 18, 20, 22, 24, 26, 28, 30, 32

Cross out each number as you use it.

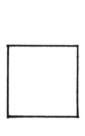

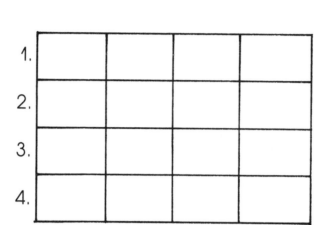

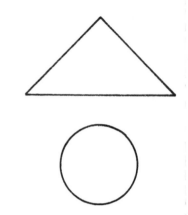

Write the lowest number of the number sequence in the bottom right space.
Write the largest number in the top left square.
Write the eighth lowest number in the right space of the second row.
Write the third largest number in the third space of the fourth row.
Write the only number divisible by eleven in the third space of the second row.
Write the second number in the sequence in the third space of the top row.
Write the fifth lowest number in the left space of the second row.
Write two times seven in the only space left in the third column.
Write the fourth largest number in the top right space.
Write the largest number that remains in the second space in the bottom row.
Write the fourth lowest number in the bottom left space.
Write the fifth highest number in the right space of the third row.
Write the third lowest number in the second space in the top row.
Write the lowest remaining number in the second space in the third row.
Write the lowest remaining number in the left space of the third row.
Write the only remaining number in the second space of the second row.
Add the numbers in row one. Write the answer in the box.
Add the numbers in the left column. Write the answer in the triangle.
Add the numbers on the diagonal from the top left space to the bottom right space. Write the answer in the circle.
Do all the other columns, rows and diagonals equal the same number? _____
Show proof of your answer.
Can you duplicate this using a different sequence? Try it.

Name _____

Co·De·Tective

A equals **2**. After that every other letter of the alphabet is an even number. (**2, 4, 6**, etc.)

B equals **1**. Every other letter after **B** is an odd number. (**3, 5, 7**, etc.)

Write the number for each letter of the alphabet under it.

A B C D E F G H I J K L M N O P Q R S T U V W X Y Z

__ __

1. _____ ___

2. _____

3. _____

_____

4. _____

_____

_____

_____

1. 24-17-10-19-6   19-7-6   13-22-14-1-6-17   16-5   10-13-4-7-6-20   10-13   2
   26-2-17-3.

2. 3-17-2-24   20-10-23   20-18-22-2-17-6-20   14-2-17-12   19-7-6   5-16-22-17-19-7
   16-13-6   24-10-19-7   2-13   23.

3. 24-17-10-19-6   19-7-6   3-2-19-6   2-13-3   26-6-2-17   16-5   26-16-22-17
   1-10-17-19-7   2-13-3   24-7-6-17-6   26-16-22   24-6-17-6   1-16-17-13.

4. 3-17-2-24   2-13   16-21-2-11   11-6-13-8-19-7-24-10-20-6   10-13   19-7-6
   14-10-3-3-11-6   16-5   19-7-6   1-16-23.   14-2-12-6   2   5-22-13-13-26
   2-13-10-14-2-11   5-17-16-14   10-19.

IF8712 Reading Skills

Far Out

Sun

Mercury _____ :

_____ Venus   Earth _____

_____ Mars

_____ Jupiter   Uranus _____

_____ Saturn   Neptune _____

_____ Pluto

Draw a line through the name of the fourth planet from the sun.
Mark an **X** on your planet.
Draw a line under the planet with rings.
Draw a circle around the seventh planet from the sun.
Make an **X** above the middle planet.
Draw a triangle around the smallest planet.
Color in Earth's neighboring planets.
Make an **X** under the planet farthest from Earth.
Draw a line through the planet second farthest from the farthest planet.
Write a capital **L** on the largest planet.
Circle the name of the hottest planet.
Cross out the word on the diagram that is not a planet's name.
Underline the names of the planets whose names are spelled with the same
    letters except one.
Number the planets alphabetically on the line next to their names.
Earth's letters can be arranged to spell two other words. What are they?

_____

Write the names of the planets in order according to their size. _____

_____

_____

Name _____

Famous Scientists

Follow the directions to write the name of each scientist.

An Astronomer	A Chemist

‾1‾ ‾2‾ ‾3‾ ‾4‾ ‾5‾ ‾6‾ ‾7‾	‾8‾ ‾9‾ 10 11 12 13 14
A Doctor	A Physicist
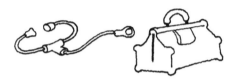	
15 16 17 18 19 20 21	22 23 24 25 26 27 28 29
A Botanist	A Mathematician
	$3+4=$ $\quad$ $\dfrac{3X \div 3}{5X + 5}$ $\quad$ $-\dfrac{12}{8}$
	9
	$\underline{X6}$
	$+ 2y - 270$
30 31 32 33 34 35	36 37 38 39 40 41

On line **33**, use the fourth letter in **crevice**.

On lines **10** and **25**, use the letter that makes the /s/ sound.

On lines **3** and **5**, use the consonant after **K** in the alphabet.

On lines **14, 17, 20, 32** and **35**, use the third letter in **agreeable**.

On line **38**, use the letter that looks like a capital M upside down.

On line **1**, use the consonant before **H** in the alphabet.

On lines **6, 12, 22, 27, 34** and **37**, use the first vowel in the third syllable of **influence**.

On line **15**, use the consonant that appears twice in **abominable**.

On lines **18, 24, 29, 36** and **41**, use the fourteenth letter of the alphabet.

On lines **2, 9, 16, 19** and **31**, use the silent letter in the second syllable of **approach**.

On lines **7** and **40**, use the letter between **N** and **P**.

On lines **4, 23** and **28**, use the fifth letter from the end of **quickly**.

On line **8**, use the silent consonant in **pneumonia**.

On lines **11, 26** and **39**, use the middle letter in **heather**.

On line **21**, use the double letter in **riddle**.

On line **30**, use the first consonant in the second syllable of **acorn**.

On line **13**, use the sixth letter from the end of the alphabet.

         IF8712 Reading Skills

Listening/Following Directions   Name _____

 **Start to Finish**

Follow the directions for each of the following sequences.

Write a number. _____   _____

Double it. _____   _____

Add 120 ÷ 30. _____   _____

Multiply by 83 − 78. _____   _____

Add a dozen. _____   _____

Multiply by a tenth of one hundred. _____   _____

Subtract 320. _____   _____

Cross out the last two digits. What is the number? _____   _____

Try this again with another number in the column at the right. _____   _____

Write a number. _____   _____

Double it. _____   _____

Add 45 − 28. _____   _____

Subtract one-third of nine. _____   _____

Divide by 54 ÷ 9 − 4. _____   _____

Subtract the original number. _____   _____

Try this again with another number in the column at the right. _____   _____

Write a number. _____   _____

Multiply it by the number of sides in a triangle. _____   _____

Add 6 × 4 ÷ 8 − 2. _____   _____

Multiply by 63 ÷ 9 − 4. _____   _____

Add the original number. _____   _____

Subtract the number of legs on a tripod. _____   _____

Cross out the last digit. What is the number? _____   _____

Try this again with another number in the column at the right. _____   _____

World Capitals

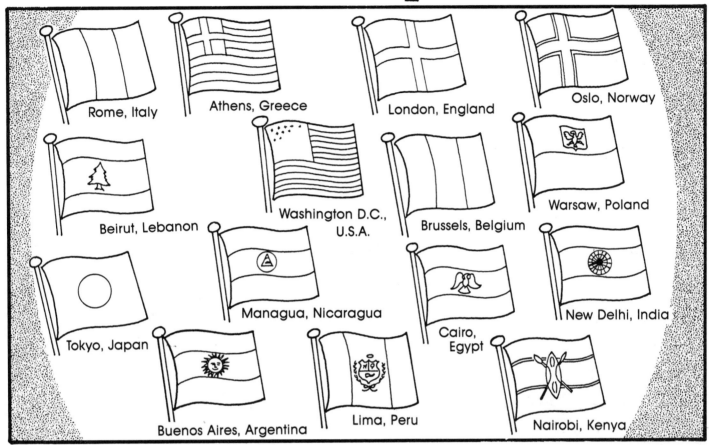

Rome, Italy

Athens, Greece

London, England

Oslo, Norway

Beirut, Lebanon

Washington D.C., U.S.A.

Brussels, Belgium

Warsaw, Poland

Tokyo, Japan

Managua, Nicaragua

Cairo, Egypt

New Delhi, India

Buenos Aires, Argentina

Lima, Peru

Nairobi, Kenya

Draw a line under each capital that:
- begins with **W**, but does not end in **W**.
- has two words in its name.
- has the same last letter as the first letter of Japan's capital.
- is the capital of a country whose name begins with **P** and ends in **U**.
- begins with the same letter as the country to which it is the capital.
- contains three **A**'s in its name.
- is the capital of an island country.
- is a homonym of a word that means to wander.
- has the same first and last letter.
- has the same name as a city in Georgia

The two capitals not underlined are _____.

On what continent are they? _____ Write the names of three other

countries on that continent. _____

Circle the names of the countries. Write their capitals in alphabetical order.

_____

_____

Sequencing

Read each sentence. Circle the two words which tell **when** something happens. Write each circled word on the correct line to show which word would come before or after the other word in time.

1. Mike hopes to someday visit Washington D.C., but meanwhile he reads books about the capital city.

    before _____ after _____

2. Some of the tourists left immediately for the airport while others planned to leave later in the day.

    before _____ after _____

3. Although John has put off mowing the yard for now, he knows he must eventually get it done.

    before _____ after _____

4. Kim said she would have arrived sooner, but she waited for a phone call that finally came.

    before _____ after _____

5. Tom wanted to appear earlier in the play, but his character did not appear until the last scene.

    before _____ after _____

6. The photographer said that Sally would have her picture taken first, but that Kevin would be next.

    before _____ after _____

Circle the word that would come before the other word. Use the circled word in a sentence.

1. eventually–previously: _____

_____

2. immediately–later: _____

_____

3. earlier–last: _____

_____

Sequencing

Timely Events

Read each sentence about two events. One event should happen before the other. Write each event on the correct line.

1. When you have completed your assignment, place your report in the basket on the teacher's desk.

   Before: _____

   After: _____

2. The golfers plan to finish the last four holes as soon as the rain stops.

   Before: _____

   After: _____

3. Before the rush hour traffic began, Ed rode his bike to the mall to buy a new pair of tennis shoes.

   Before: _____

   After: _____

4. After returning from a visit to his aunt and uncle's ranch, Paul wrote them a long thank you letter.

   Before: _____

   After: _____

5. The day after his twenty-first birthday, Meg's cousin inherited fifty thousand dollars.

   Before: _____

   After: _____

6. The scouts collected money for a month to buy clothes and toys for needy kids.

   Before: _____

   After: _____

Sequencing

Name _____

Look What I've Made!

Read each invention on the time line. Write **1–15** to put the dates in order. Write each date by an invention starting from the earliest to the latest date.

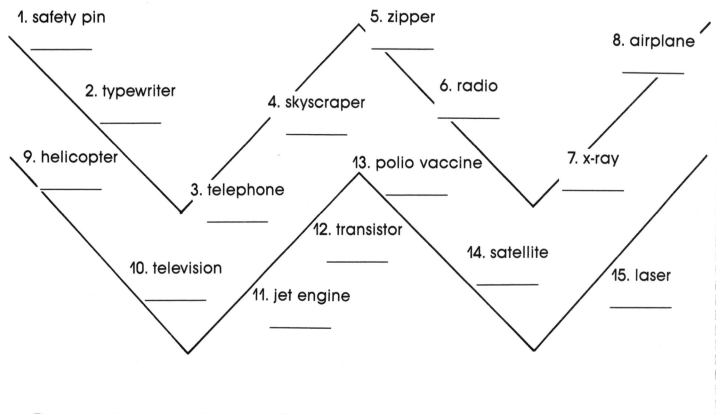

1. safety pin _____
2. typewriter _____
9. helicopter _____
3. telephone _____
10. television _____
11. jet engine _____
4. skyscraper _____
5. zipper _____
13. polio vaccine _____
12. transistor _____
6. radio _____
14. satellite _____
7. x-ray _____
8. airplane _____
15. laser _____

◯ 1907 ◯ 1884 ◯ 1920 ◯ 1849 ◯ 1960 ◯ 1903 ◯ 1876 ◯ 1893
◯ 1957 ◯ 1895 ◯ 1952 ◯ 1895 ◯ 1867 ◯ 1947 ◯ 1939

Write **before** or **after** on each line.

The **transistor** was invented _____ the **laser**.

The **polio vaccine** was invented _____ the **x-ray**.

The **helicopter** was invented _____ the **airplane**.

The **jet engine** was invented _____ the **safety pin**.

The **radio** was invented _____ the **television**.

The **zipper** was invented _____ the **typewriter**.

The **telephone** was invented _____ the **skyscraper**.

Name _____

Hail to the Chief!

Selecting a president of the United States can be a very elaborate process. It officially begins in the summer of the election year when the two major parties (Democrats and Republicans) hold their conventions. They each select a candidate for president and vice president. During the next few months, the candidates campaign across the country. Then on the first Tuesday following the first Monday of November, the election is held. Shortly thereafter, the Electoral College meets to confirm the winner. Early in January, after the election in November, members of Congress meet to officially count the Electoral College votes. On January 20th, Inauguration Day, the elected president takes the same oath of office that was taken by George Washington.

*Write **1-6** to put the major presidential election events in the correct order.

◯ Inauguration   ◯ Campaign   ◯ Electoral College

◯ Election   ◯ Nomination   ◯ Congress Confirms

On the lines below, write the specific steps (in order) in electing a president of the United States.

1 _____

2 _____

3 _____

4 _____

5 _____

6 _____

Sequencing

 # Perfect Party Planners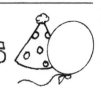

Below is a list of tips for planning a perfect party. Find the four tips that go under each heading. Write each set in the correct order on the lines.

☐ Make a grocery list.
☐ Introduce all the guests.
☐ Buy the decorations.
☐ Put away uneaten food.
☐ Choose the party theme.
☐ Prepare food for party.
☐ Take down decorations.
☐ Welcome guests to party.

☐ Decorate party area.
☐ Place food on table just before guests arrive.
☐ Wash the dishes.
☐ Shop for party food.
☐ Congratulate yourself for a great party.
☐ Make a list of party supplies.
☐ Plan the party menu.
☐ Enjoy the party, too.

 # Perfect Party

Party Decorations

1 _____
2 _____
3 _____
4 _____

Party Food

1 _____
2 _____
3 _____
4 _____

The Party

1 _____
2 _____
3 _____
4 _____

After the Party

1 _____
2 _____
3 _____
4 _____

Name _____

Chef's Shuffle

Read the recipe carefully. Write **1–15** in the circles to put the cooking steps in the correct order.

Chocolate Soufflé

Break 3 ounces of German chocolate into pieces. Mix with 2 tablespoons of cold coffee. Place in the upper part of a double boiler and place over hot water on the stove. Stir until melted. Cool for 10 minutes.

Preheat oven to 325 degrees. Butter a 1½ quart soufflé dish. Separate 6 egg whites from the yolks. Beat egg whites until stiff. Add a dash of salt. Gradually add sugar and stir slowly. Add the cooled chocolate mixture and mix thoroughly. Pour into the soufflé dish. Place in oven and bake for 30–35 minutes. Serve immediately.

○ Mix chocolate with 2 tablespoons of cold coffee.

○ Add the cooled chocolate mixture and mix.

○ Butter a 1½ quart soufflé dish.

○ Cool mixture for ten minutes.

○ Add a dash of salt.

○ Break 3 ounces of German chocolate into pieces.

○ Serve immediately.

○ Beat the egg whites until stiff.

○ Preheat oven to 325 degrees.

○ Pour mixture into soufflé dish.

○ Place mixture in double boiler and place over hot water.

○ Add sugar to egg whites and stir slowly.

○ Separate 6 egg whites from the yolks.

○ Stir chocolate mixture until melted.

○ Place in oven and bake for 30–35 minutes.

Name _____

What's Inside?

Read each book title. The titles give strong clues about the contents of the books. Choose each title that indicates that the book deals with sequencing. Write those titles on the lines.

A 10-Step Plan to Improve Grades	A Checklist for Summer Camp	Mysterious Cove
The Century's Top 20 Events	My Ordeal on Mt. McKinley	A Listing of the Top 10 Colleges
Crazes Over the Decades	Space Exploration: Past to Present	Steps in Saving Money
Our Natural Resources	Sports Greats: Year to Year	Transportation Through the Ages
Benjamin Franklin	American History 1800–1950	Paul Revere

1. _____

2. _____

3. _____

4. _____

5. _____

6. _____

7. _____

8. _____

9. _____

10. _____

Sequencing

As the World Turns...

Read each major event in world history. Write each event in the correct order under the heading. (B.C. comes before the other dates. To put B.C. dates in order, count backwards. **Ex: 2500 B.C.** happened before **338 B.C.**)

206 B.C.—The Great Wall of China built. **1920**—Panama Canal opened. **1945** —United Nations founded. **27 B.C.**—Augustus is first Roman emperor. **768**— Charlemagne rules the Franks. **1914**—World War I begins. **1815**—Napolean defeated at Waterloo. **1865**—U.S. Civil War ends. **1750 B.C.**—Babylonian Empire begins. **1000**—Ericson sails to America. **1869**—Suez Canal opened. **1440**—Invention of moveable type. **1969**—Man walks on the moon. **331 B.C.**— Alexander the Great defeats Persians. **1192**—The first shogun rules Japan. **1920**—League of Nations established. **1500 B.C.**—Shang dynasty rules China. **1522**—Magellan sails around world. **1492**—Columbus discovers America. **1279** —Kublai Khan conquers China.

Famous World Events

Ancient Times (B.C. dates)

_____ : _____
_____ : _____
_____ : _____
_____ : _____
_____ : _____

Middle Ages (476–1450)

_____ : _____
_____ : _____
_____ : _____

Early Modern Times (1450–1900)

_____ : _____
_____ : _____
_____ : _____
_____ : _____

Modern Times (1900–   )

_____ : _____
_____ : _____
_____ : _____

Name _____

Look Where I've Been!

Read the list of explorations. **Write 1-14** to put the events in sequence from the earliest to the most recent.

____ In September of 1513, Vasco de Balboa discovered the Pacific Ocean.

____ Eric the Red sailed from Iceland to Greenland in 982.

____ In 1535, Jacques Cartier sailed up the St. Lawrence River.

____ Robert Perry reached the North Pole in 1909.

____ In 1498, Vasco Da Gama reached India by sea.

____ Hernando Cortes conquered what is now Mexico in November of 1519.

____ In 1963, Valentina Tereshkova became the first woman in space.

____ James Cook explored the South Pacific in 1768.

____ In September of 1519, Ferdinand Magellan set sail to begin a voyage around the world.

____ William Clark crossed the Rocky Mountains in 1804.

____ In April of 1513, Ponce de Leon landed in Florida.

____ Christopher Columbus sailed to America in 1492.

____ In 1969, Neil Armstrong became the first man on the moon.

____ Sir Edmund Hillary explored the South Pole in 1957.

Complete each statement with name(s) from above.

_____ and _____ were explorers **before** James Cook.

_____ was an explorer **after** Sir Edmund Hillary.

_____ and _____ were explorers **after** Ponce de Leon.

_____ was an explorer **before** William Clark.

_____ was an explorer **before** Columbus and _____ was **after** him.

A Passport to Travel

At some time, you may decide to leave the country to travel in other countries. As an American citizen, you are free to leave the country at anytime. But to enter another country or re-enter the United States, you must have an official passport that identifies you as an American citizen. So, before you travel out of the country you will need to obtain a passport in the following way.

First, you must obtain an official copy of your birth certificate. Next, you must have your photo taken. It can be black and white or color, but it must be two inches by two inches in size. If you are not old enough for a driver's license, you will need a copy of your parent's license. Then you must obtain and fill out an official passport application form. Next, you should return the birth certificate, photo, driver's license and application to the passport office. You will then be asked to pay a fee for making your passport. The passport office will then process your information. Soon, you will obtain an official passport which will identify you as a citizen of the United States of America.

Rewrite the sentences on the lines to put the "steps to a passport" in order.
- Obtain and fill out an official passport application.
- Pay fee for passport.
- Obtain a copy of your birth certificate.
- You will have a United States passport.
- Passport office will process the information.
- Have a copy made of parent's driver's license.
- Return birth certificate, photo, license and application.
- Have a 2 x 2 inch photo taken.

1. _____

2. _____

3. _____

4. _____

5. _____

6. _____

7. _____

8. _____

Vocabulary

Name _____

Write the words in the box after their appropriate category.

frilly	unctuous	southeast	slither	pantry
reptiles	artist	depressed	adorned	luxurious
underhanded	inclined	rodents	gourmet	exhilarated
tricky	skimmed	affectionate	elaborate	insects
tramp	straight	deceitful	center	markers
acrylics	skyward	pastels	amble	culinary

Decorative Words _____

Directional Words _____

Kitchen Words _____

Words That Can Bite _____

Words for Feelings _____

Words That Draw _____

Words That Move _____

Slippery Words _____

A word is missing in each sentence below. Select a sensible word from above. Write it on the line in the sentence where it belongs.

1. The boat _____ over the water to win the race.

2. The furnishings in the display house bedrooms were as _____ as a lamb's curly hair.

3. Mary usually uses _____ because they look similar to, but are easier to use than oil paints.

4. Ted was _____ to take the path to the right although the directions said to go left.

5. The floor's surface had an _____ covering after it was polished.

6. Our dog always gets _____ when he sees us packing suitcases.

7. Dad is a _____ because he enjoys cooking and eating fine food.

8. The _____ were especially annoying after the rain.

Vocabulary

Name _____

Occupations

Use the letters in each flower petal plus the letter in the flower's center to name occupations.

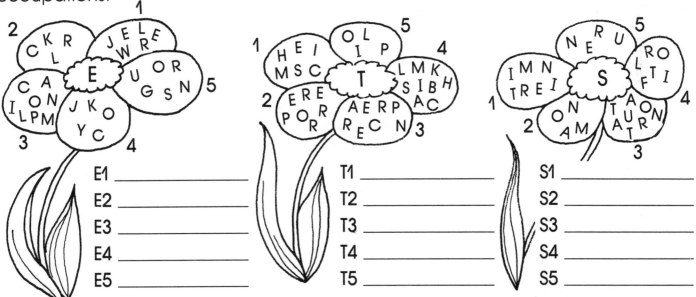

E1 _____	T1 _____	S1 _____
E2 _____	T2 _____	S2 _____
E3 _____	T3 _____	S3 _____
E4 _____	T4 _____	S4 _____
E5 _____	T5 _____	S5 _____

With which occupation above are the following associated?

starting gate _____   a scalpel _____

cash register _____   tickets and cuffs _____

metals and gems _____   acids and beakers _____

saws and nails _____   paper and pencil _____

maps and compass _____   anvil and fire _____

a pulpit _____   a capsule _____

stones and bricks _____   ribbons and wires _____

thermometer _____

Fill in the occupations in the sentences below.

The _____ assisted the _____ during the operation.

The _____ hired the _____ to help sell his wares and a _____ for protection.

The _____, _____ and _____ may work together on a building.

Many _____ were _____ before entering the space program.

A _____ makes shoes for the horses _____ ride.

_____ are considered snoopy and pushy by some citizens, but it is part of uncovering the news.

                   IF8712 Reading Skills

Vocabulary

 Paired Sense

Add one letter to each word below to form pairs of antonyms.

___ealthy	___ickly	___mart	___tupid
___arm	___old	___iser	___pender
___ight	___ark	___aised	___owered
___cared	___rave	___assive	___light
___egin	___top	___onest	___rooked
___and	___cean	___alter	___ersist
___ront	___ack	___riend	___nemy

Write the pair of antonyms that will fit in each sentence.

The veterinarian cared for the _____ dog until he was _____ again.

Some people would rather drive over _____ and sail over the _____ than fly in a plane.

The workmen _____ their supplies over their heads before they _____ them to the level on which they were working.

The amount of food was so _____ that no one noticed the _____ tear in the tablecloth.

The _____ boy climbed out on the limb of the tree to rescue

the _____ cat.

Harry ran in the _____ door and out the _____ to get away from the angry bee.

On very _____ nights, we sit by the fire to keep _____ .

When Kurt wants something, he _____ and does not _____ .

My _____, Josh, plays basketball on the _____ team.

You may _____ the test now and do not _____ until I tell you.

The _____ employee was caught stealing by an _____ employee.

For a _____ person, he was _____ to think that no one would steal from the open safe.

The _____ night had turned _____ when the moon came out from behind the clouds.

I borrow from my sister, a _____, because I am a _____ and cannot save a thing.

Vocabulary

Name _____

Write two rhyming words to fit each definition.

Example: beautiful cat _pretty kitty_____

red flower _____   chef's novels _____

slippery fowl _____   cube timepiece _____

plump dog _____   drowned animal _____

dark tan hat _____   restful tree_____

strange buck _____   cozy insect _____

The word you write below must fit the definition and rhyme with the given word. The first letters will form a column that will spell a "Witty Ditty".

Something to eat and it rhymes with shaken   ___ _____

A noise and it rhymes with crumble   ___ _____

A measurement and it rhymes with pinch   ___ _____

A word for "chow" and it rhymes with club   ___ _____

A group of animals and it rhymes with bird   ___ _____

Another word for "hobo" and it rhymes with champ   ___ _____

To be a little unsure about something and it rhymes

with cheery   ___ _____

A mischievous fellow and it rhymes with blimp   ___ _____

A supernatural being and it rhymes with roast   ___ _____

Covered with fur and it rhymes with merry   ___ _____

A word meaning pull behind and it rhymes with crowed ___ _____

What is the new "Witty Ditty"? _____

Write a definition for it. _____

27

Vocabulary

Comparisons

A simile compares things which have something in common and still are often quite different. One thing is compared with another using **as** or **like**.

Jane is stubborn as a mule.

A metaphor states the comparison even stronger.

Jane is a mule.

Jane is not a mule, but she is stubborn. A characteristic of mules is their stubbornness. It is this characteristic that is being compared.

Complete the following similes.

as sharp as a _____   climbs like a _____

as jumpy as a _____   shines like a _____

as thin as a _____   sounds like a _____

as strong as a _____   moves like a _____

as tenacious as a _____   talks like a _____

Do not use any of the verbs or adjectives from above as you continue.

as _____ as a ghost   _____ like a snake

as _____ as ice   _____ like a powder puff

as _____ as a bear   _____ like falling leaves

as _____ as a feather   _____ like a bird

as _____ as honey   _____ like a rusty gate

Write three sentences. Use a simile in each one to describe as directed.

The appearance of a roof _____

The size of a cut _____

The color of the sky _____

Draw a line under the metaphors in the sentences below.

The river was a fence around the pasture.
Sandra's nose was bent out of shape when she was not elected class president.
The loss of her dog broke Kristen's heart.
Grandma's arthritic fingers were all thumbs when it came to opening small jars.
They sat on a time bomb waiting for the results of the medical tests.

Vocabulary

It Figures...

Idioms say one thing, but mean something else. Use the meanings listed below. Write the number of each meaning on the line next to the sentence in which the idiom it defines is used.

1. Rumors circulate quickly
2. Elated
3. In a quandry
4. Acted in a determined way
5. Twenty-four hours continuously
6. Lost the opportunity
7. Wildly disruptive
8. Made a foolish remark
9. Forgave each other
10. Believe only half of what is said
11. A forecast that something bad will occur
12. Rough times
13. Got angry
14. Got married
15. Really sad
16. Talk together

____ John was **in the dark** about what to fix for dinner.

____ The class was **bouncing off the wall** when the substitute told them to take their seats.

____ Michael and Karen finally **tied the knot** last Friday.

____ Henry **missed the boat** when he turned down a job in the White House.

____ Gale really **put her foot in her mouth** when she met the new neighbor.

____ John **took the bull by the horns** when he saw two boys beating a stray cat.

____ The graduating class was **flying high** after their final exams.

____ Terry had some **hard knocks** growing up in the big city.

____ Mom always **chews the fat** with the neighbor after everyone has gone in the morning.

____ Fido waited **around the clock** for his master to return from a business trip.

____ The entire school was **down in the dumps** after they were defeated by their closest rival.

____ Sandy **lost his cool** when he missed the last bus.

____ Although **the handwriting was on the wall**, Emily went ahead with her plans.

____ Justin and Marty **buried the hatchet** once the debate was settled.

____ **Tongues were wagging** when the principal was seen talking to several students.

____ You have to **take** what you hear **with a grain of salt**.

Vocabulary

Name _____

Oops! Look Alikes!

```
L  O  T  S  T  A  R  T
A  T  B  A  T  T  E  R
B  R  N  O  N  I  G  A
O  U  T  O  R  R  A  P
R  B  L  U  E  E  L  O
S  L  A  C  K  S  O  N
```

Find the word in the puzzle that will fit into two sentences below.
Circle it and write it where it belongs.
(The word only appears once in the puzzle, but it will be used twice below.)

1. Mother prepared the __batter__ for pan-cakes.
2. The wind messed up the _____ in my hair.

3. Wally was really _____ when his dog was struck by a car.
4. Sean's pet _____ can say "hello", "good-bye" and "I like you".
5. Molly tried out for the leading _____ in the spring play.
6. The __batter__ struck out for the second time.
7. The boys' _____ meets every other Tuesday in Seth's tree house.
8. A _____ bird built a nest in the hole of the old oak tree.
9. The gang had a _____ they used to beat down the door.
10. The meeting was a total _____ .
11. Tina's little brother likes to _____ everything she says.
12. Charles _____ right through the wall with the screwdriver.

Write the sentence number in which the homograph being defined is located.

____ a bird   ____ imitate   ____ implement
____ mixture of flour, eggs and milk   ____ separation   ____ drill
____ a baseball player   ____ dull   ____ color
____ sad   ____ organization   ____ role

Write the homograph from the box to the right that can have either meaning.

drawing of earth; plan in detail _____

chirp; peek through narrow opening _____

land along river's edge; place to keep money _____

small piece of paper; game _____

tall grass; mouthpiece for a woodwind instrument _____

REED	PEEP
MAP	
TAG	BANK

Vocabulary

Name _____

Oops! Sound Alikes!

Write the homophone or homonym for the following:

kernel _____   naval _____

bald _____   quarts _____

need _____   fair _____

patients _____   jam _____

vain _____   earn _____

idle _____   you _____

liar _____   read _____

Write two homophones or homonyms for the following:

scents _____ two _____ rain _____

there _____ way _____

Use a homophone or homonym pair from above in each sentence.

The _____ woman was upset when a _____ became raised on her hand.

What is the _____ for entrance to the _____?

The _____ choked on a _____ of corn.

The _____ said he could play the _____ when he couldn't.

The _____ officer's _____ was injured when he fell from the deck onto the dock.

Nursing requires a great deal of _____ when caring for many _____ .

George had to _____ a lot of money to buy the _____ his mother wanted for her birthday.

We _____ to _____ the dough before we let it rise.

The _____ man _____ when he saw his new car roll into the path of an oncoming truck.

Vocabulary

Noun and Verb Clusters

Write the answers to the definitions in the squares around the corresponding number. The words will connect with each other. All but one of the answers go in a clockwise direction.

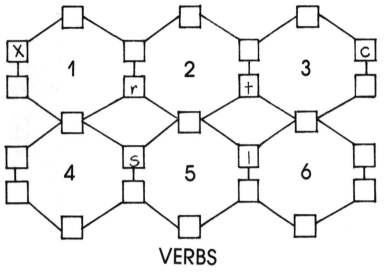

VERBS

1. Send out of the country
2. Turn around
3. Go after with force
4. Provide with free sweets
5. Choose
6. Go from place to place

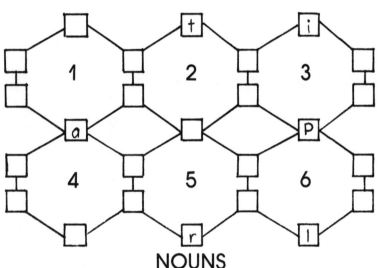

NOUNS

1. A piece of farm machinery
2. Person who buys and sells
3. Church community
4. A fruit
5. Piece of hair, string or yarn
6. Supernatural being

Use the words above to fill in the blanks in the sentences below.

South America _____ _____ to other parts of the world.

The mysterious _____ seemed to _____ at midnight.

People _____ far to attend the _____ in Green County.

It was difficult to _____ the right _____ of yarn to finish the sweater.

The _____'s back wheels _____ in reverse in wet mud.

The _____ often _____ his customers to milk and cookies.

 IF8712 Reading Skills

Simply Amazing H's

Read each paragraph. Put one line under the sentence which tells the main idea. Put two lines under the sentences which tell supportive ideas. Put a check by the best title for the paragraph.

Heart: The heart is probably the most amazing and efficient machine in existence. It pumps blood through sixty thousand miles of arteries, veins and capillaries. During a lifetime, it will pump enough blood to fill the fuel tanks of over two thousand 747 jet planes.

☐ The Heart Pumps Gallons of Blood
☐ The Heart: An Incredible Machine
☐ A Lifetime Pump

Height: As we sleep, our bodies grow taller. The discs in our spine absorb fluid like a sponge, making the spine longer. While awake the liquid is squeezed out as we stand and move, causing the spine to shorten again.

☐ Moveable Spines
☐ Sleepwalking
☐ Taller in Our Sleep

Handedness: Most people in the world are right-handed. An average of 91 percent of the world's population uses their right hand mainly. From studying ancient art, scientists believe that this was true in ancient times, too.

☐ A Right-Handed World
☐ Ancient Handwriting
☐ How Most People Write

Name _____

Read each list below. Decide what the best heading for each list would be. Write the heading on the line.

_____

1. Finding a four-leaf clover
2. Carrying a rabbit's foot
3. Finding a penny heads up
4. Sleeping with a silver dollar under your mattress
5. Finding a horseshoe

_____

1. Loveland, Oklahoma
2. Lovelady, Texas
3. Lovejoy, Illinois
4. Love, Mississippi
5. Lovepoint, Maryland

_____

1. Los Angeles Dodgers
2. New York Mets
3. Chicago Cubs
4. St. Louis Cardinals
5. Cleveland Indians

_____

1. Reese's Pieces
2. Snickers
3. Butterfinger
4. Almond Joy
5. 3 Musketeers

_____

1. There are almost 2 billion children in the world.
2. In the U.S., one out of every 1,000 children works.
3. 1 billion children in the world do not finish elementary school.
4. Over 250 million children in the world are poor.
5. It can cost over $150,000 to raise a child to age 18.

_____

1. Captain Kirk
2. Doctor McCoy ("Bones")
3. Mr. Spock
4. Lt. Uhura
5. Chekhov

Complete the list of:
    5 Ways Kids Can Make a Better World

1. _____   2. _____

3. _____   4. _____

5. _____

Name _____

I Didn't Know That!

Read each paragraph. Put a check by the **main idea**. Underline two **supportive ideas** in the paragraph. On the line, write an appropriate title for each.

_____

In 1974, an attempt was made to communicate with alien intelligence thousands of light years away. From an observatory in Puerto Rico, a powerful radar beam was used to broadcast a three-minute message into outer space. It will take 50,000 light years to receive a reply, if there is one.

Radar's best use is for alien communication.

Radar beams have given us a chance to explore other life in the universe.

_____

Perhaps the most incredible tunnel system ever built was constructed in Vietnam during their war with France. Called the Cu Chi network, it stretched for 150 miles. The tunnel system, which took thirty years to build by hand, contained a hospital, livestock and thousands of soldiers.

An elaborate tunnel system was built by hand in Vietnam.

The Cu Chi network of tunnels is now used for traveling.

_____

Time capsules are an intriguing way of leaving a record of our time for the future. One time capsule was buried in 1964 at the World's Fair in New York. It contains among other things: a Bible, freeze-dried food, a Beatles' record and an electric toothbrush. It is to be opened in 5000 years!

Time capsules should contain important objects.

Time capsules can leave clues of our culture to the future.

Fascinating Facts

Read each paragraph. The main idea is somewhere in the paragraph. It may be at the beginning, middle or end of the paragraph. Find and underline the main idea in each paragraph. Put a check by the best title for each paragraph.

By studying rapid eye movements during sleep, scientists have discovered dreaming patterns of humans and animals. Cold-blooded animals such as fish and reptiles do not dream. Warm-blooded animals such as mammals and birds do dream.

☐ Dreams of Mammals
　　☐ Patterns of Dreaming
　　　☐ Rapid Eye Movements

On a sunny day, the gleam from the World Trade Center in New York City can be seen two states away. The center contains enough concrete to form a path from New York to Washington, D.C. It has enough electrical wire to reach Mexico. It even has its own zip code. The New York City World Trade Center is one of the tallest buildings in the world.

☐ An Incredible View
　　☐ From New York to Mexico
　　　☐ An Amazing Building

The first recorded Siamese twins were born in 945 A.D. Throughout history other Siamese twin births have been recorded. Siamese twins occur in as few as one in 200,000 births. Born in the Kingdom of Siam in 1811, Chang and Eng are two of the most famous twins.

☐ Siamese Twins
　　☐ Chang and Eng
　　　☐ Twin Births

wow!

Name _____

The Fact of the Matter

Read each paragraph. Put one line under the main idea. Put two lines under the sentences which tell supportive ideas. In your own words, write the main idea on the line.

Shorthand

Shorthand, a system of quick writing, has been used since the year 63 B.C. A Roman named Marcus Tiro invented a system which remained in use for over 600 years. One of the symbols & is still used today.

main idea: _____

money

The world's oldest money was issued in China in 2697 B.C. The bank notes were called "flying money" or convenient money. It was printed on paper made from the mulberry tree. Blue ink was used.

main idea: _____

hibernation

Animal hibernation is one of nature's most amazing mysteries. Bears can sleep for five months without eating or drinking. Other animals, such as woodchucks, squirrels and some reptiles, sleep so soundly that they can be picked up and tossed without waking them.

main idea: _____

elephants

A white elephant is considered a symbol of good luck in Thailand. It is a law that any white elephant found in Thailand must be given to the king. White elephants are really gray elephants which have pink eyes.

main idea: _____

Drawing Conclusions

Name _____

I Would Conclude...

Read each fact below. Put a check by the correct conclusion on each line. Write another conclusion for each fact.

1.  Only one person is known to have ever been hit by a meteorite.

☐ Meteorites usually fall in forests, lakes or hills.
☐ The chances of being hit by a meteorite are almost zero.

2. A "jiffy" is defined as one hundred thousand billion billionths of a second.

☐ A jiffy is an incredibly short period of time.
☐ A jiffy is enough time for a quick phone call.

3.  President George Washington died on the last hour of the last day of the last week of the last month of the last year of the eighteenth century (1700's).

☐ President Washington died December 7, 1799.
☐ President Washington died December 31, 1799.

4.  An average golf course requires at least 400,000 gallons of water a week to stay green.

☐ A golf course is heavily watered twice a week.
☐ It takes a tremendous amount of water to keep a golf course green.

5.  Killer bees have been responsible for killing almost three hundred persons in Brazil since 1957.

☐ Killer bees are especially threatening to people in Brazil.
☐ Killer bees pose a worldwide threat to people.

Drawing Conclusions

Name _____

Yesterday to the Future

Use the three calendars to help fill in each blank below.

year _____

S	M	T	W	T	F	S
						1
2	3	4	5	6	7	8
9	10	11	12	13	14	15
16	17	18	19	20	21	22
23	24	25	26	27	28	

1900

S	M	T	W	T	F	S
				1	2	3
4	5	6	7	8	9	10
11	12	13	14	15	16	17
18	19	20	21	22	23	24
25	26	27	28			

year _____

S	M	T	W	T	F	S
		1	2	3	4	5
6	7	8	9	10	11	12
13	14	15	16	17	18	19
20	21	22	23	24	25	26
27	28	29				

1. Each of the calendars shows the second month of the year. That month is

_____ .

2. The first and third months are 100 years before and after 1900. Write the year above each month.

3. In this year, Valentine's Day (Feb. 14) would come on a Wednesday. The year must be _____ .

4. In this year, the month would begin and end on the third day of the week. The year is _____ .

5. In this year, the month would begin on the last day of the week and end on the sixth day of the week. The year is _____ .

6. In the year 2000, George Washington's birthday would come exactly two weeks from February 8th. What day of the month and day of the week is it?

_____

7. In the year 1900, Abraham Lincoln's birthday would be two days before Valentine's Day. What day would his birthday be? _____

8. In the year 1800, what day of the week would the last day of January come on? _____

9. In the year 2000, what day of the week would the first day of March come on? _____

10. The 8th, 15th and 22nd days of the month are on Thursday. The year is

_____ .

11. If you had a birthday on the fourth Wednesday of February in the year 2000, what would your birthday be? _____

12. Every four years is Leap Year which adds a day to February. The year _____ would be a Leap Year.

Cause and Effect

Cause and Effect

Read each sentence. Put a line under something that happened. (effect) Put two lines under the cause. Write **1** and **2** by **cause** and **effect** to tell their order in the sentence.

1. The museum opening was delayed for two weeks because they were waiting for the ancient artifacts to arrive.

   _____ cause   _____ effect

2. Everyone was relieved when the artifacts arrived safely because they could so easily have been damaged in their crates.

   _____ cause   _____ effect

3. Because the artifacts were breakable, they were placed behind glass cases so no one could touch them.

   _____ cause   _____ effect

4. Because the artifacts were valued as priceless, the museum hired extra security guards to protect them.

   _____ cause   _____ effect

5. Many people traveled from other cities and states to see the ancient exhibit because it had never been shown in this country.

   _____ cause   _____ effect

6. Due to public demand, the museum decided to stay open each night from eight o'clock until eleven o'clock.

   _____ cause   _____ effect

7. Special brochures and photos were available to the public because everyone wanted to learn as much as possible about the exhibit.

   _____ cause   _____ effect

8. Because the artifacts exhibit was such a success, other museums asked for permission to show the exhibit, too.

   _____ cause   _____ effect

Cause and Effect

Name _____

That's Why!

Read each sentence. Write two different things which <u>may</u> have caused the event in each sentence to happen.

1. **Effect:** The train had left the station just before Jeff arrived.

   Cause I: *Jeff's car broke down.* _____

   Cause II: _____

2. **Effect:** The star basketball player could not play in the second half.

   Cause I: _____

   Cause II: _____

3. **Effect:** The line of cars came to a sudden stop on the narrow road.

   Cause I: _____

   Cause II: _____

4. **Effect:** The teacher returned Bob's paper and asked him to redo it.

   Cause I: _____

   Cause II: _____

5. **Effect:** The tourist stopped in the city to buy a new map.

   Cause I: _____

   Cause II: _____

6. **Effect:** Kate's mother stopped for gas on the way to the game.

   Cause I: _____

   Cause II: _____

7. **Effect:** Tom called Kevin to ask what their homework assignment was.

   Cause I: _____

   Cause II: _____

8. **Effect:** Meg was late for cheerleader practice Saturday morning.

   Cause I: _____

   Cause II: _____

Portrait Possibilities

Look at the portrait of the lady. Write **15** possibilities about the lady and her life that you feel must be true.

1 _____   8 _____

2 _____   9 _____

3 _____   10 _____

4 _____   11 _____

5 _____   12 _____

6 _____   13 _____

7 _____   14 _____

15 _____

Inference

 **Autograph Please?**

Read each book title in column **B**. Read the list of professions in column **A**. Write a letter on each line to tell which person probably wrote each book.

A

___ 1. a heart doctor

___ 2. a biologist

___ 3. a concert pianist

___ 4. a lawyer

___ 5. a salesperson

___ 6. a school principal

___ 7. an historian

___ 8. a tennis player

___ 9. a movie actor

___ 10. a comedian

___ 11. a veterinarian

___ 12. a politician

___ 13. a news reporter

___ 14. an astronomer

___ 15. a banker

B

a. Today's Education: A New Approach

b. Our Body's Amazing Pump

c. Behind My Presidential Campaign

d. 10 Ways to Make Them Say "I'll Buy It"

e. Trial Tips

f. Let's Have Healthier Pets

g. Secrets of the Universe

h. Game, Set, Match!

i. Laugh 'Til I Cry!

j. Chopin: His Life and His Music

k. Money Wise

l. A Nose for News

m. Plant and Animal Life of the Arctic.

n. Heroes of the American Revolution

o. Hollywood Hints

Read each professional name below. Write the title of a book which could be written by each.

I. a sportscaster _____

II. a computer designer _____

III. an electrician _____

IV. a gardener _____

V. a mystery writer _____

Name _____

See the U.S.A.

Read the table of contents from **See the USA**. Read each sentence taken from the book. Write the chapter and page number on each line to tell from where the quote is probably taken.

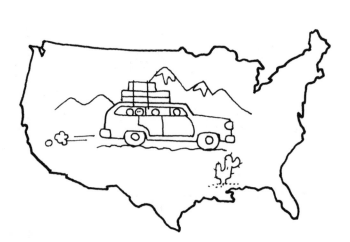

Ch. ___ page ___ Rolling clothes in plastic bags will prevent wrinkles.

Ch. ___ page ___ Some state parks will rent tents at a reasonable rate.

Ch. ___ page ___ Many wilderness parks exist in the northwest U.S.

Ch. ___ page ___ Traveler's checks are recommended for safety.

Ch. ___ page ___ Neat, clean rooms at a very reasonable rate

Ch. ___ page ___ Many airlines offer discounts for families.

Ch. ___ page ___ Allow two rolls of film for each sightseeing day.

Ch. ___ page ___ The southeast U.S. is especially lovely in the springtime.

Ch. ___ page ___ Some suites offer whirlpools in the bathrooms.

Ch. ___ page ___ Special maps with trails marked can be ordered.

Ch. ___ page ___ Proper diet and enough rest will help you enjoy your trip.

Ch. ___ page ___ Backseat games for children will help prevent boredom.

Ch. ___ page ___ Some roads offer safety lanes for bikers.

Inference

Details Tell!

Look at each person. Write a sentence that tells what each detail tells about the person's personality, life, habits, interests, etc.

1. A. _____

   B. _____

2. A. _____

   B. _____

3. A. _____

   B. _____

4. A. _____

   B. _____

5. A. _____

   B. _____

6. A. _____

   B. _____

Fact and Fantasy

Read each sentence. Underline **fact** or **fantasy** to describe each sentence. If the sentence is a fact, rewrite the sentence as fantasy. If the sentence is fantasy, rewrite the sentence as a fact. At the beginning of each new sentence, write **fact** or **fantasy**.

1. **fact or fantasy:** Every four years an election is held to elect a President of the United States.

   _____ : _____

2. **fact or fantasy:** The Grand Canyon only appears to exist since it is really a mirage formed by waves of heat from the earth.

   _____ : _____

3. **fact or fantasy:** The United States is bordered on the east and west by the Atlantic and Pacific Oceans and by Canada and Mexico on the north and south.

   _____ : _____

4. **fact or fantasy:** The bottom of the ocean floor provides the ceiling for a hidden continent that lies under it.

   _____ : _____

5. **fact or fantasy:** As the cutter chopped each Christmas tree down, a larger more beautiful tree appeared in its place.

   _____ : _____

6. **fact or fantasy:** The famous Alamo still stands in San Antonio, Texas.

   _____ : _____

Fact and Fantasy

Fact or Fantasy

Read each sentence. If it is a **fact**, circle the letter in column **A**. If it is a **fantasy**, circle the letter in column **B**. Write each circled letter on a line below.

	A	B
1. At midnight, the island submerges in the water and then rises again.	g	w
2. Newspapers, TV and radio are some ways of learning the daily news.	r	k
3. Hydrogen and oxygen are names of gases.	i	b
4. Four feet of new fallen snow covered the desert.	q	t
5. The basketball player used special powers to make the ball go in the basket.	m	e
6. Many families go on a vacation during the summer months.	v	x
7. Dogs are believed to be spirits of ancient people.	c	f
8. The hula hoop and pogo stick were popular fads.	a	r
9. When blown, the whistle had the power to make everything stop.	h	c
10. Computers can only do what they are programmed to do.	n	j
11. When the man turned sideways, he could disappear.	p	s

___ ___ ___ ___ ___   ___ ___ ___ ___   ___ ___ ___ ___ ___ .
 1   2   3   4   5   7   3   6   5   7   8   9   4   11

1. _____
2. _____
3. _____
4. _____
5. _____

___ ___ ___ ___ ___   ___ ___ ___ ___   ___ ___ ___ ___ ___ ___ ___ ___ ___ .
 1   2   3   4   5   7   3   6   5   7   8   10 4   8   11 3   5   11

1. _____
2. _____
3. _____
4. _____
5. _____

47

Fact and Opinion

Facing the Facts

Some facts stay the same, while others may change. Read each fact below. On each line, write **can change** or **cannot change**.

1. _____ Sam's baby brother has two teeth.
2. _____ The United States is north of the equator.
3. _____ Jere's father and mother are 38 years old.
4. _____ The whale is the world's largest mammal.
5. _____ Kathleen has 697 stamps in her collection.
6. _____ The football uniforms are covered with mud.
7. _____ Molly has three overdue books from the library.
8. _____ Carrie is the oldest child in her family.
9. _____ Lettuce, potatoes and beans are vegetables.
10. _____ Steve's birthday is October 21st.
11. _____ The Earth has one moon in its orbit.
12. _____ The Harris family lives in Denver, Colorado.

In the circles below, write each number of a fact from above that can change. Write a sentence about how it can change.

◯ _____
◯ _____
◯ _____
◯ _____
◯ _____
◯ _____

Fact and Opinion

City Sights

Look at the scene below. Write **ten facts** and **ten opinions** about this city scene.

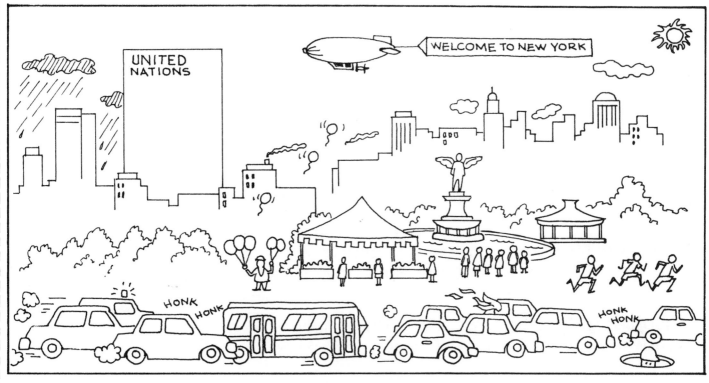

Facts

1. _____   2. _____
3. _____   4. _____
5. _____   6. _____
7. _____   8. _____
9. _____   10. _____

Opinions

1. _____   2. _____
3. _____   4. _____
5. _____   6. _____
7. _____   8. _____
9. _____   10. _____

Fact and Opinion

Name _____

The lawyer is asking the witnesses many questions. Some of the answers are facts, some are opinions. The judge will only accept facts. Read each question and answer. Write **fact** or **opinion** on the lines by the names to describe their answers.

1. **question:** Mr. Wallace, what was the stranger wearing?
   answer: He was wearing a blue coat, red scarf, black slacks and black shoes.

_____

2. **question:** Miss Raines, did you recognize the intruder?
   answer: How could I? He wore glasses so he wouldn't be recognized.

_____

3. **question:** Mr. Henry, what did you hear from your window?
   answer: I heard a sound that must have been the intruder breaking in.

_____

4. **question:** Ms. Harris, what time did you notice the broken lock?
   answer: It was 10:15 p.m., just as I arrived home.

_____

5. **question:** Mrs. Patterson, do you know the owner of the stolen painting?
   answer: He is the nicest boss I have ever worked for.

_____

6. **question:** Mr. Samuels, was the painting insured?
   answer: Yes, the painting was insured for ten thousand dollars.

_____

7. **question:** Miss Ryan, did you see the defendant take the painting?
   answer: Of course he took it! It had to be him.

_____

Mr. Wallace _____ Miss Raines _____ Mr. Henry _____

Ms. Harris _____ Mrs. Patterson _____ Mr. Samuels _____

Miss Ryan _____

*On the line under each answer, write another answer to the question. If the answer is a fact, write an opinion. If it is an opinion, write a fact.

Fact and Opinion

Name _____

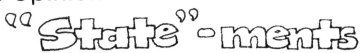

Read each sentence about a state(s). On each line, write **fact** or **opinion** to describe each sentence.

_____ 1. Alaska and Texas (a)re the two largest states in the U.S.

_____ 2. Flori(d)a is the best state for a summer vacation.

_____ 3. Georgia is the largest state east of the Mississippi Ri(v)er.

_____ 4. Hawaii is the only state completely surro(u)nded by water.

_____ 5. Col(o)rado has the nation's best ski slopes.

_____ 6. Sacramento is the state capital of Califor(n)ia.

_____ 7. The desert(s) of Arizona are beautiful to paint.

_____ 8. Minnesota's northern border (i)s next to Canada.

_____ 9. Wyoming has the friend(l)iest people in the U.S.

_____ 10. New York Cit(y) is not the capital of New York state.

_____ 11. Kansas and Nebraska are located in the mid(w)est.

_____ 12. Texas has the best state parks.

_____ 13. R(h)ode Island is the smallest state.

_____ 14. It is (e)asy to find a job in Kentucky.

_____ 15. New Jersey is called the Garden S(t)ate.

Use the circled letters from above to write the question.

__ __ __ __   __ __ __ __ __   __ __   __ __ __   __ __ __ __   __ __ ?
11 13 1 15   7 15 1 15 14   2   5   10 5   4   9   8   3   14   8   6

_____

Write three facts and three opinions about **your** state.

Facts
1. _____
2. _____
3. _____

Opinions
1. _____
2. _____
3. _____

Following Directions

Name _____

Follow the directions to write the name of each artist responsible for each work of art.

$\overline{14}$ $\overline{7}$ $\overline{5}$ $\overline{12}$ $\overline{7}$ $\overline{10}$ $\overline{1}$ "The Entombment"	$\overline{14}$ $\overline{10}$ $\overline{9}$ $\overline{4}$ $\overline{14}$ $\overline{7}$ $\overline{11}$ $\overline{16}$ $\overline{6}$ "The Night Watch"
$\overline{2}$ $\overline{7}$ $\overline{11}$ $\overline{8}$ $\overline{13}$ $\overline{8}$ $\overline{12}$ "Sunflowers"	$\overline{9}$ $\overline{15}$ $\overline{3}$ $\overline{12}$ $\overline{10}$ $\overline{1}$ $\overline{7}$ $\overline{11}$ $\overline{8}$ $\overline{10}$ $\overline{1}$ $\overline{13}$ "Pieta"
$\overline{16}$ $\overline{7}$ $\overline{2}$ $\overline{15}$ $\overline{11}$ $\overline{3}$ $\overline{15}$ "The Last Supper"	$\overline{10}$ $\overline{1}$ $\overline{8}$ $\overline{14}$ $\overline{10}$ $\overline{3}$ $\overline{13}$ "The Burial of Count Orgaz"

1. Use the first consonant after the second vowel in **ITALY**.
2. Use the fifth consonant from the end of the alphabet.
3. Use the consonant that comes just after the two vowels together in **MASTERPIECE**.
4. Use the ninth letter before the eighth consonant in the alphabet.
5. Use the letter that comes just after the fourth vowel in the alphabet.
6. Use the consonant in **ART** that appears last in the alphabet.
7. Use the vowel that appears twice in **CANVAS**.
8. Use the fifth letter after the second vowel in **PAINTING**.
9. Use the consonant that comes between two vowels in **FAMOUS**.
10. Use the vowel that appears twice in the second syllable of **FLORENCE**.
11. Use the consonant that comes between the second vowel and third consonant in **PAINTER**.
12. Use the sixteenth consonant from the end of the alphabet.
13. Use the vowel in **SCULPTOR** which appears first in the alphabet.
14. Use the consonant which appears before and after the fourth letter in **PORTRAIT**.
15. Use the third vowel in **RENAISSANCE**.
16. Use the letter between the second consonant and second vowel of the alphabet.

     IF8712 Reading Skills

Name _____

They're ~ Noteworthy! ♪

Follow the directions for each sentence.

1. _ _ _ _ _ _   _ _ _ _ _ _ _ _ _   _ _ _ _, a famous
   a o n J n h   a e i a b t S n s   a h c B
   4 2 5 1 6 3   8 2 7 4 3 6 1 9 5   2 4 3 1
composer and organist, was the father of twenty children.

♪ Unscramble the musician's name. _____
♪ Circle the synonym for well-known.
♪ Use the letters in his middle name to write three other words. Write them
   above his last name.
♪ Over the eighth word, write the name of two other musical instruments.
♪ Multiply the number of children times your age. Write the answer over the
   family word which applies to Bach.

2. _ _ _ _ _ _ _ _   _ _ _ _ _ _ _   _ _ _ _ _ _ was a
   l g W g f a o n   u d s e A a m   z M r a t o
   3 5 1 8 4 6 2 7   6 4 7 5 1 3 2   3 1 5 4 6 2
child genius who composed and performed his own music at the age of
five.
Unscramble the musician's name. _____
♪ Put a dotted line under the synonym for brilliant person. ♪
♪ Total the number of letters in his first and middle names. _____
♪ Divide by the last word in the first sentence. Write his last name this many
   times above his first name.
♪ Circle the antonym for adult. Write another "age" term over the circled
   word.

3. _ _ _ _ _ _ _ _   _ _ _ _ _ _ , a brilliant pianist from the
   r e i d c F e r   o n p C i h
   2 3 7 4 8 1 5 6   3 6 4 1 5 2
age of eight, wrote over 200 compositions in his lifetime.
♪ Write a synonym for the twelfth word in the above sentence. _____
♪ Circle the number word. Above it write two other number words with the
   same number of letters.
♪ Unscramble the musician's name. _____
♪ Above the number 200, write the year it will be 200 years from now.
♪ Use the letters in the last word to write three new words over his first name.

 IF8712 Reading Skills

Following Directions

Name _____

Tic-Tac-Trivia

Read each "Trivia" question. Write each answer in the correct puzzle space. Then select the correct category for each question. Draw the symbol in the box in each puzzle space. Find the symbols which form a "Tic-Tac-Trivia" line. Draw a line.

I : SPORTS   **X**: TV   **Ɛ**: CURRENT EVENTS   **O**: SCIENCE
+: HISTORY   **✓** : GEOGRAPHY

I.

1.	2.	3.
4.	5.	6.
7.	8.	9.

II.

1.	2.	3.
4.	5.	6.
7.	8.	9.

I. 1. What sport has the World Series?
2. Who was president during the Civil War?
3. Who was Batman's partner?
4. Hawaii floats in what ocean?
5. The U.S. president's first name?
6. Who is a famous cartoon rabbit?
7. What planet is famous for its rings?
8. A game where you hit the "birdie" over the net.
9. How many brothers did Beaver Cleaver have?

II. 1. What is one of the leading U.S. political parties?
2. Who is the star of the Tonight Show?
3. What is the invisible line that circles the Earth's middle?
4. What is the body's pump?
5. The Empire State Building is in what state?
6. Cleopatra was queen of what country?
7. What is the famous river found in South America?
8. Which sport has the Super Bowl?
9. Who cried "The Redcoats are coming"?

Following Directions

They're Ancient History Now!

Follow the directions for each sentence.

1. The ancient _ _ _ _ _ _ _ _ _ _ _ _ built a magnificent city,
   a s b n n B a l i y o
   2 11 3 7 10 1 9 5 8 4 6
   Babylon, which was the religious, trading and artistic center of their
   civilization.
   Unscramble the name.
   Put a dotted circle around the antonym for ordinary.
   Above the fifteenth word, write two examples of art.
   Use the letters in the last word to write three new words above the
   synonym for construction.
   Circle the first four letters of the eighth word.
   Write an antonym for this word above the third word.

2. The ancient _ _ _ _ _ _ _ were ruled by dynasties, a series of
   e i e C n h s
   5 3 7 1 4 2 6
   rulers from the same family, some of which lasted for 1000 years.
   Unscramble the name.
   Put a sequence of six X's above the synonym for sequence.
   Multiply the number of zeroes in 1000 times the number of vowels in
   the seventh word. Write the number over the antonym for modern.
   Under the third word containing six letters, write three names of your
   family members.
   Over the synonym for governed, write the current U.S. President's name.

3. The ancient _ _ _ _ _ _ worshipped many gods, including Zeus
   e s G e k r
   3 6 1 4 5 2
   who was believed to have lived on Mount Olympus, site of the original
   Olympic Games.
   Unscramble the name.
   Put two lines under the synonym for location.
   Above the next to the last word, write three Olympic sports.
   Circle the antonym for copied.
   Over the third capitalized word, write the name of another Greek god
   in capital letters.

Following Directions

Name _____

Follow the directions to show the routes traveled.

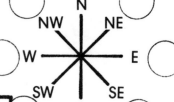

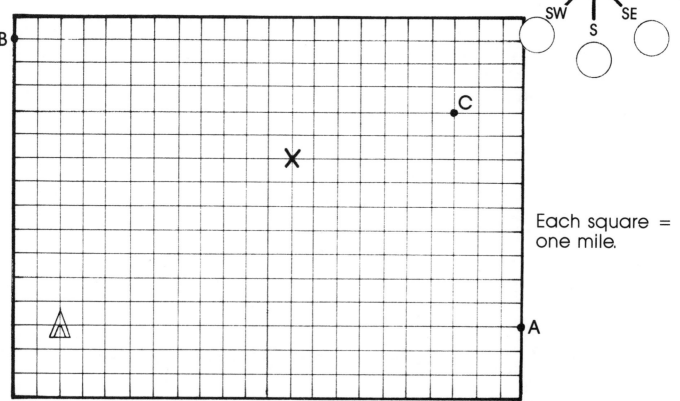

Each square = one mile.

Beth **(A)** and Paul **(B)** are planning to meet at the campsite **(X)**.
Draw a line:

B: Go **2** miles east and **4** miles south. Mark a ✳.
A: Go **3** miles northwest and **2** miles west. Mark a ⊙.
B: Go **3** miles southeast and **4** miles northeast. Mark a ◿.
A: Go **3** miles west and **2** miles southwest. Mark a †.
B: Go **3** miles northeast and **5** miles south.
A: Go **3** miles northwest and **3** miles northeast.

Beth and Paul should now be at the campsite. **(X)**
Together, they are to rendezvous with Kim. **(C)**

AB: Go **5** miles northeast, **3** miles south and **2** miles east.

Beth, Paul and Kim are now together. They will travel to the new campsite.

ABC: Go **4** miles southwest and **5** miles west. Mark a Z.
ABC: Go **3** miles northwest and **5** miles south. Mark a ↗.
ABC: Go **5** miles southwest and **2** miles north.

Beth, Paul and Kim are now at the new campsite.
Total the number of miles traveled in each direction.
Write each number in the ◯ by each direction ✳ above.

Following Directions

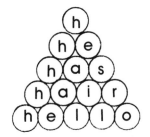

Name _____

Choose a letter for the top circle in each pyramid. Write a word beginning with that letter to fill in each level of the pyramid. It may be a two, three, four, five or even six-letter word. You may use names, too.

I.

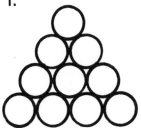

II.

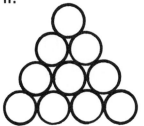

III.

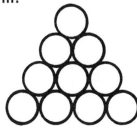

IV.

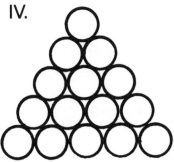

V.

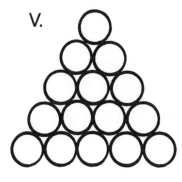

VI.

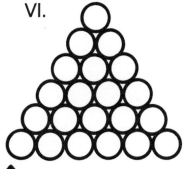

VII.

VIII.

△ Can you make a **7, 8, 9** and **10-letter** pyramid?

Name _____

L	U	T	W	Q	M	A	V	I	X	K	H	O	C
I	X	E	E	B	I	Q	P	P	A	E	U	Z	O
N	A	K	R	Y	R	Z	W	M	O	N	D	A	Y
C	V	E	R	B	A	L	I	Z	E	N	N	T	H
O	E	L	E	K	G	R	M	B	T	E	F	H	T
L	N	B	R	I	E	L	P	G	Y	D	I	I	J
N	I	F	R	A	C	T	I	O	N	Y	F	R	S
F	C	M	I	L	L	I	O	N	M	R	T	T	S
J	E	D	V	T	H	U	R	S	D	A	Y	Y	N

Find and mark each word in the following way:

1. **Find:** The thirty-fifth president of the U.S. elected in 1960.
   Write: 35 on any three letters in the name as long as one is a vowel.

2. **Find:** A word that rhymes with **summarize** which means "to voice a thought."
   Write: An **X** on the last three letters.

3. **Find:** A famous European city built on water canals.
   Write: The chemical sign for water - H_2O - on each letter.

4. **Find:** A word for a desert "sight" which really does not exist.
   Write: A cactus symbol 🌵 on the **1st, 2nd, 5th** and **6th** letters.

5. **Find:** One of the presidents carved on Mt. Rushmore in 1941.
   Write: The total of the numbers in **1941** on each letter.

6. **Find:** A synonym for **mistake**.
   Write: The correct letter in the square which contains the incorrect letter.

7. **Find:** A math term for a "part of a whole."
   Write: A different example of this term on each letter.

8. **Find:** The day of the week that the **24th** would come on if the first day of the month came on Tuesday.
   Write: **24** on every letter that also appears in Tuesday.

9. **Find:** How many sides you would have if you totaled the sides in **6** triangles and **3** squares.
   Write: The total number backwards on the first and last letters.

10. **Find:** The number you would get by adding a zero to one hundred thousand.
    Write: The total number of zeroes on each letter.

     IF8712 Reading Skills

Following Directions

Name _____

Not (Just) a Single Clue

Look at the scene of the crime below. The investigator must make a complete list of suspicious clues in the house. Read each item on the list. Find the clue in the scene. Write the correct letter in the circle. List the specific location for each clue. Name room, location in room (direction) and specific place in room. Ex: Spilled ink: Study, west wall, top of table.

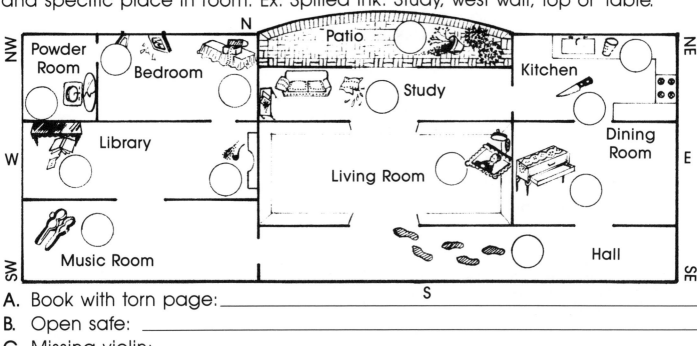

A. Book with torn page: _____

B. Open safe: _____

C. Missing violin: _____

D. Pipe tobacco: _____

E. Muddy footprints: _____

F. Knife: _____

G. Missing silver: _____

H. Fingerprints on glass: _____

I. Torn pillow: _____

J. Missing jewels: _____

K. Broken pot: _____

L. Cracked mirror: _____

M. Broken window: _____

Place **5** more mysterious clues in the house. Write the name, location and position of each.

1. _____

2. _____

3. _____

4. _____

5. _____

Follow the directions to create the names of the first and last states to officially enter the United States.

Write the word **FIRST**.   _____

Change the second consonant to the
   twelfth letter of the alphabet.   _____

Change the vowel to the last vowel
   in **STATE**.   _____

At the end of the word, add the first word
   in the compound word **WAREHOUSE**.   _____

Cross out the letter that appears three
   times in **CONSTITUTION**.   _____

Change the third consonant from the end
   to the second vowel from the beginning
   of the word.   _____

Change the first letter to the eighth letter
   in **INDEPENDENCE** to discover the name
   of the **first** state.   _____

Write the word **LAST**.   _____

Change the third letter to the fourth letter
   from the end of the alphabet.   _____

Cross out the third consonant.   _____

Add the vowel that is found in the middle
   of **STATE** to the end of the word   _____

At the end of the word, add all of the
   vowels that are found in **HIKING**.   _____

Change the first letter to the last letter
   in **FIFTIETH** to discover the name of
   the **last** state.   _____

Target Practice

Ex: II-3 =
Target II -
Ring **3**

Write **T** in the space shared by **II-I** and **III-3**.
Write **A** in the space shared by **V-2** and **IV-2**.
Write **R** in the space shared by **I-3**, **II-1** and **III-3**.
Write **G** in the space shared by **I-3** and **III-1**.
Write **E** in the space shared by **I-3**, **II-3** and **III-2**.
Write **T** in the space shared by **III-3** and **IV-3**.
Write **P** in the space shared by **I-1** and **III-3**.
Write **R** in the space shared by **II-3** and **III-3**.
Write **A** in the space shared by **I-2**, **II-3** and **III-3**.
Write **C** in the space shared by **IV-1** and **V-3**.
Write **T** in the space shared by **I-2** and **III-2**.
Write **I** in the space shared by **IV-3** and **V-2**.
Write **C** in the space shared by **I-3** and **II-2**.
Write **E** in the space shared by **IV-3** and **V-1**.

Alphabetize to Capital-ize!

Write **1-6** to put each international city in alphabetical order.

A. ◯Beirut ◯Brasilia ◯Madrid ◯Milan ◯Lima ◯Perth

B. ◯Tokyo ◯Ottawa ◯Oslo ◯Stockholm ◯Sidney ◯Rome

C. ◯Athens ◯Bagdad ◯Cairo ◯Alexandria ◯Bonn ◯Canton

D. ◯Vienna ◯Perth ◯Warsaw ◯Venice ◯Wellington ◯Paris

E. ◯Nairobi ◯Naples ◯Mexico City ◯Moscow ◯New Delhi ◯Mecca

F. ◯Paris ◯Peking ◯Jerusalem ◯Lagos ◯London ◯Florence

Use the code of letters and numbers above to find the name of each capital.

_____, France
F-5

_____, England
F-4

_____, Kenya
E-4

_____, Brazil
A-2

_____, Canada
B-2

_____, Sweden
B-5

_____, Germany
C-4

_____, Israel
F-2

_____, Spain
A-4

_____, Poland
D-5

_____, Austria
D-4

_____, Egypt
C-5

_____, Mexico
E-2

_____, Peru
A-3

_____, Greece
C-2

_____, Italy
B-3

_____, India
E-6

_____, Japan
B-6

_____, Russia
E-3

_____, New Zealand
D-6

_____, Nigeria
F-3

Directionally Speaking

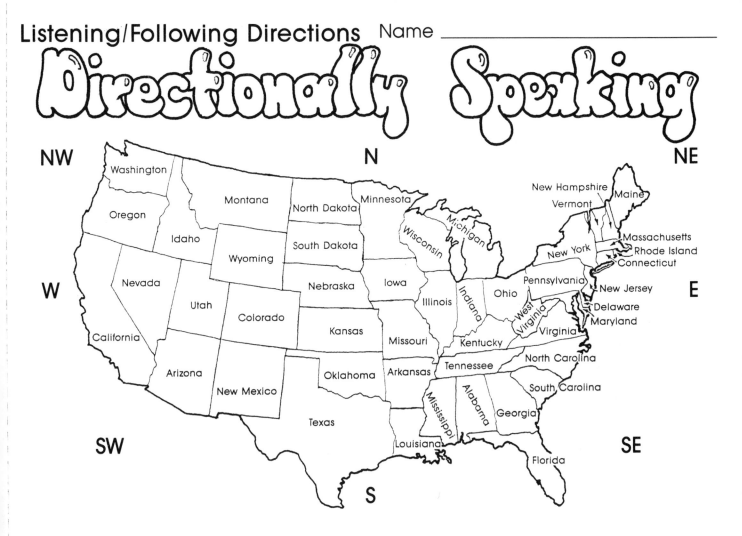

1. Traveling from northern Texas west to southern California, you would go through two states. Under each state's name, write the number of letters in each name.
2. If you stood at the southeast corner of Utah, you would touch the southwest corner of another state. Write that state's name on the state just north of New Mexico.
3. Write the number of letters in Ohio on that many states southeast of it.
4. Locate the first three states directly south of North Dakota. If **A-L = 8** and **M-Z = 6**, add the value of each state. Write each total on the state directly east of each state.
5. Use the letters in the most northwest state (other than Alaska) to make 5 new words. Write the words just east of the most northeast state.
6. Multipy the number of **E's** times the number of **S's** and **N's** in the name of Tennessee. Write that number in each state that touches Tennessee to the north, east and south.
7. Find each state west of Kansas whose name begins with a vowel. Write the states' names in alphabetical order on the state southwest of Arkansas.
8. Put your initials on your state. Find any other state whose name has the same number of letters as your state. If it is northeast, east, southeast or south of your state, write your initials on it in small letters. If it is southwest, west, northwest or north, write your initials in capital letters.

Alpha - Bet You Can Do This!

A B C D E F G H I J K L M N O P Q R S T U V W X Y Z

	1	2	3	4
1				
2				
3				
4				

4-1   1-1   4-1   1-2   3-3

4-1   3-2   2-4   1-4   2-2   3-1   2-1

3-4   4-4   1-2   4-3

2-3   4-4   3-2   1-3   4-2   2-2   3-2   3-1

4-2   1-1   4-4   3-4   4-1   1-4 !

Follow the directions below to find the correct letter for each box.

Ex: 2-4 = down 2, across 4

3-3 : Write the third letter after the twenty-second letter.

4-1 : Write the ninth letter before the eleventh consonant.

2-3 : If the alphabet were numbered **1-26**, write the letter you would have for the answer to **36 ÷ 12**.

1-4 : Write the letter between the eleventh and thirteenth letters.

3-4 : Write the letter that is eight letters after the next to the last vowel.

2-1 : Write the letter that comes between the third vowel and the seventeenth consonant from the end.

1-2 : If you start with A and count every other letter, write the letter which comes between the ninth and tenth letters.

4-3 : Skipping all vowels, write the letter which comes nineteenth from the end of the alphabet.

1-1 : Write the sixth consonant after the fourth vowel.

3-2 : Write the letter which comes between the tenth consonant and the second vowel from the end.

4-2 : Write the letter which comes just before the twenty-first consonant from the end.

2-4 : If the alphabet were numbered **1-26** starting at the end, write the letter you would have for the answer to **100 ÷ 5**.

3-1 : Write the ninth consonant after the third vowel.

4-4 : Skipping the first five letters, write the second letter after the seventh consonant.

1-3 : Write the fifth consonant after the fourth vowel.

2-2 : Write the nearest vowel to the ninteenth letter from the end.

• Now, write the correct letter on each line to find the answer to the puzzle.

Know Thyself!

One Great Kid!

Write **1-6** to alphabetize the words in each line. Write the fifth word in alphabetical order on the correct lines below. Complete each answer.

⭐ A ◯signal ◯sign ◯signature ◯silence ◯sift ◯sight

⭐ B ◯ceremony ◯centipede ◯cent ◯century ◯cement ◯central

⭐ C ◯pastei ◯pastime ◯past ◯paste ◯pasta ◯pastry

⭐ D ◯graduate ◯graceful ◯gracious ◯grain ◯grab ◯grade

⭐ E ◯charades ◯chapter ◯chant ◯channel ◯characteristics ◯chap

⭐ F ◯tailor ◯talents ◯tactic ◯tailspin ◯talk ◯taffy

⭐ G ◯wayside ◯wavy ◯weakness ◯wealth ◯way ◯wattage

⭐ H ◯forecast ◯forest ◯forego ◯forceful ◯foreign ◯football

⭐ I ◯amateur ◯ambition ◯amass ◯amble ◯always ◯amazing

⭐ J ◯admire ◯admiral ◯adept ◯adjust ◯adjective ◯admit

1. The person whom I most _____ is _____.
   J

2. My _____ is _____.
   A

3. My _____ is to be a _____.
   I

4. At the turn of the next _____, I will be _____ years old.
   B

5. My favorite _____ is _____.
   C

6. I will _____ from high school in the year _____.
   D

7. My worst _____ is _____.
   G

8. My best _____ are _____.
   E

9. My _____ are _____.
   F

10. The _____ country I most want to visit is _____.
    H

Listening/Following Directions   Name _____

Size 'em Up!

Write **C** on the left leg of the second tallest boy.

Write **Y** between the third tallest girl and the second tallest boy.

Write **L** above the shortest boy.

Write **A** on the third tallest boy's right hand.

Write **S** on the tallest boy's left ear.

Write **O** between the two people closest to the third tallest boy.

Write **E** on the shirt of the person between the second tallest boy and the shortest boy.

Write **T** above the third person from the tallest boy.

Write **P** on right shoe of the third tallest girl.

Write **H** between the two people between the third tallest girl and the shortest boy.

Write **I** on the face of the third tallest person.

Write **M** above the second shortest person.

  2   9   7   14   1   6   13   4   15   8   3   12   10   11   5

On line **5**, write the letter on the second tallest person.

On line **7**, write the letter between the third tallest girl and the second tallest boy.

On lines **9** and **3**, write the letter above the shortest boy.

On line **6**, write the letter on the person by the third tallest boy.

On lines **15** and **10**, write the letter above the person between the second tallest boy and the shortest boy.

On line **1**, write the letter on the person next to the tallest boy.

On line **4**, write the letter on the hand of the third tallest boy.

On line **2**, write the letter between the shortest boy and the second tallest girl.

On lines **12** and **11**, write the letter on the tallest person.

On line **13**, write the letter on the second person from the tallest boy.

On line **8**, write the letter between the second tallest boy and the tallest girl.

On line **14**, write the letter above the second shortest person.

Name _____

Read the recipe carefully. Write **1 - 15** in the circles to put the cooking steps in the correct order.

Tantalizing Tacos

In a large skillet, melt a tablespoon of butter over medium heat. Sauté 1/2 cup of chopped onions. Add a pound of ground beef and cook until brown. Add one eight-ounce can of tomato sauce. Add 1/4 teaspoon of chili powder. Add 1/4 teaspoon of salt. Add 1/4 teaspoon of garlic salt. Stir the seasoned meat mixture well and cook over low heat for 15 minutes.

While the meat mixture cooks, shred a pound of cheese. Chop a small jar of green olives. Chop 3 tomatoes and 1/2 a head of lettuce. Chop one bunch of green onions.

Heat 10 taco shells. Fill each half-full with meat mixture. On top, add cheese, lettuce, tomatoes, olives and onions.

◯ Chop 3 tomatoes and 1/2 a head of lettuce.

◯ Add 1/4 teaspoon of salt.

◯ In a skillet, melt a tablespoon of butter over medium heat.

◯ Chop a bunch of green onions.

◯ Stir well and cook over low heat for 15 minutes.

◯ Add one eight-ounce can of tomato sauce.

◯ On top, add cheese, lettuce, tomatoes, olives and onions.

◯ Add 1/4 teaspoon of garlic salt.

◯ Add a pound of ground beef and cook until brown.

◯ Heat 10 taco shells.

◯ Add 1/4 teaspoon of chili powder.

◯ Saute 1/2 cup of chopped onions.

◯ Chop a small jar of green olives.

◯ Fill taco shells half-full with meat mixture.

◯ While the meat mixture cooks, shred a pound of cheese.

Name _____

To Become a Citizen...

If you were born in the U.S. or born to citizens of the U.S., you are automatically a citizen of the U.S. If you are not a citizen and desire to become one, you must follow this procedure. First, you must obtain an application form, fingerprint card and biographical information form from the Immigration and Naturalization Service. Next, you must complete the forms according to specific instructions. Return the forms to the Immigration and Naturalization Service. You will then be informed of an appointment date to meet an examiner to discuss your application. You must take two witnesses who are U.S. citizens to the meeting with you. After the meeting, you must wait at least 30 days before a final hearing in court. At the hearing, you may be asked questions about the U.S. If the court decides you can become a citizen, you must take an Oath of Allegiance to the U.S.

☆ Rewrite the sentences on the lines to put the steps in order.

- Return the forms to the Immigration and Naturalization Service.
- At the hearing, you may be asked questions about the U.S.
- Take two witnesses who are U.S. citizens to the meeting with you.
- Obtain an application form, fingerprint card and biographical information form.
- You must take an Oath of Allegiance to the U.S.
- You must wait at least 30 days before a final hearing in court.
- Complete the forms according to specific instructions.
- The court will make a decision about your application.
- You will be informed of an appointment date to discuss your application.

1._____
2._____
3._____
4._____
5._____
6._____
7._____
8._____
9._____

Sequencing

B.C. dates are counted backwards, unlike our present-day dates which are counted forward.

Ex. The year 3500 B.C. came **before** the year 858 B.C. Read the list of B.C. events. Write **1 – 19** to put the events in sequence from the earliest to the most recent.

_____ Homer writes the Iliad in 800 B.C.

_____ In 1750 B.C., Hammurabi's Code was accepted.

_____ The Appian Way was built in 312 B.C.

_____ In 1500 B.C., iron was discovered.

_____ The Olympic Games began in 776 B.C.

_____ In 4000 B.C., the horse was domesticated.

_____ The Babylonian Empire fell in 539 B.C.

_____ In 650 B.C., coins were invented.

_____ The Julian Calendar was established in 45 B.C.

_____ In 3600 B.C., a form of writing was first used.

_____ The transmission of the alphabet occurred in 1250 B.C.

_____ In 3300 B.C., bronze was invented.

_____ Geometry was formally developed in 300 B.C.

_____ In 2400 B.C., the camel was domesticated.

_____ The Persians invaded Greece in 470 B.C.

_____ In 2550 B.C., the Great Pyramid was built.

_____ Caesar conquered Gaul in 58 B.C.

_____ In 3500 B.C., the wheel was used.

_____ The Parthenon was built in 447 B.C.

Name two events from above that occurred **before** Homer wrote the Iliad.

1. _____

2. _____

Name two events from above that occurred **after** the Persians invaded Greece.

1. _____

2. _____

Sequencing

Name _____

A Shift in Time

Read each sentence about two events. One event should happen first and the other event second. Write each event on the correct line.

1. The day after school was out for the summer, Kim and her family moved to Texas.

   First:_____

   Second: _____

2. Before leaving for work, Mrs. Harris scraped ice and snow from the windshield.

   First:_____

   Second: _____

3. Pat's class is planning a trip to the capital when they graduate from junior high.

   First:_____

   Second: _____

4. Craig worked hard all summer to earn enough money to buy a new bike.

   First:_____

   Second: _____

5. The landscapers dug and mulched the gardens before planting seeds for new flowers.

   First:_____

   Second: _____

6. Before continuing his speech, the speaker sipped water and cleared his throat.

   First:_____

   Second: _____

Name _____

Freedom Facts

Read each event in the **Revolutionary War**. Write each event in the correct order under the correct heading.

Sept. 23, 1779 — John Paul Jones captured British ship "Serapis."
Apr. 19, 1775 — Minutemen fought Redcoats at Lexington and Concord.
Jan. 3, 1777 — Washington gained victory at Princeton.
Dec. 4, 1782 — The British left Charleston.
Oct. 7, 1780 — American frontiersmen stormed the British on King's Mountain.
Mar. 7, 1776 — The British evacuated Boston.
Oct. 19, 1781 — Cornwallis' forces surrendered at Yorktown.
July 3, 1775 — Washington becomes commander of Continental Army.
Dec. 19, 1777 — Washington's men began their winter at Valley Forge.
Sept. 3, 1783 — U.S. and England sign final peace treaty.
Feb. 6, 1778 — U.S. and France become allies.
June 17, 1775 — British troops win the Battle of Bunker Hill.
July 11, 1782 — The British evacuated Savannah.
Sept. 15, 1776 — The British occupied New York City.
Dec. 29, 1778 — The Redcoats entered Savannah.

Revolutionary War Highlights

1775 – 1776

_____ : _____
_____ : _____
_____ : _____
_____ : _____
_____ : _____

1777 – 1779

_____ : _____
_____ : _____
_____ : _____
_____ : _____
_____ : _____

1780 – 1783

_____ : _____
_____ : _____
_____ : _____
_____ : _____
_____ : _____

Sequencing

Book titles give strong clues about the contents of books. Some titles can indicate that the book deals with some kind of sequence. **Ex: Ten Steps to Better Tennis**

Read each sentence. Use a "sequence phrase" below to write a title for each book.

A Listing of . . .	Year to Year	Steps in . . .
Through the Ages	Top Ten . . .	A Five-Step Plan . . . .
A Checklist . . .	Past to Present	1960 – 1980

1. This book is about kinds of music.

2. This book is about favorite desserts.

3. This book is about U.S. Presidents.

4. This book is about popular TV shows.

5. This book is about space exploration.

6. This book is about scientific discoveries.

7. This book is about training animals.

8. This book is about learning to water-ski.

9. This book is about traveling to South America.

Name _____

Each sentence tells of two things that happened. The order of the events in the sentence may or may not be the order in which they happened. In each sentence:
   Put one line under the event that happened first.
   Put two lines under the event that happened second.
On each line, write **1-2** or **2-1** to tell the order of events in the sentence.

1. ___ ___ Before mowing the yard, Paul changed to old clothes and sneakers.

2. ___ ___ Just after Sarah started to shower, the phone rang.

3. ___ ___ The football team was honored at a banquet after they won the championship game.

4. ___ ___ By the time they had reached the theater, the movie had already begun.

5. ___ ___ Shortly after the lights were dimmed, the orchestra began the concert.

6. ___ ___ Before going back to camp, the hikers poured water on their campfire.

7. ___ ___ The escaped prisoner was free for two days before he was captured.

8. ___ ___ After visiting several animal hospitals, Kevin decided to become a veterinarian.

9. ___ ___ The museum exhibit was flown to Paris at the end of its New York show.

10. ___ ___ The spectators ran indoors just before the thunderstorm began.

On the lines below, write four sentences, each with two events in the following order:

1 – 2 _____

2 – 1 _____

1 – 2 _____

2 – 1 _____

Sequencing

Washington Lifenotes

Below is a list of highlights of George Washington's life. Write **1 – 18** on the lines to put the events in order.

George Washington

_____ **Oct. 19, 1781** : Victory at Yorktown.

_____ **Dec. 3, 1792** : Re-elected President of the United States.

_____ **Jan. 6, 1759** : Married Mrs. Martha Dandridge Curtis.

_____ **July 18, 1749** : Became official surveyor in Virginia.

_____ **July 9, 1755** : Ambushed by French and Indians.

_____ **June 15, 1775** : Elected Commander of Continental Army.

_____ **Dec. 14, 1799** : Died at Mount Vernon at age 67.

_____ **Oct. 28, 1753** : Carried British ultimatum to French.

_____ **Feb. 22, 1732** : Born in Westmoreland Country, Virginia.

_____ **July 4, 1798** : Became Commander of U.S. Army.

_____ **July 3, 1754** : Surrendered Fort Necessity in French and Indian War.

_____ **Sept. 19, 1796** : Published Farewell Address refusing third term.

_____ **Feb. 5, 1751** : Made only trip out of U.S. — to Barbados Island.

_____ **Mar. 4, 1775** : Elected delegate to Second Continental Congress.

_____ **Feb. 18, 1789** : Elected first United States President.

_____ **Aug. 20, 1755** : Commanded Virginia's frontier troops.

_____ **May 25, 1787** : Became president of Constitutional Convention.

_____ **Sept. 3, 1774** : Elected delegate to First Continental Congress.

Sequencing

Building Blocks

Read the names of architectural styles through the ages. Write **1 – 15** to put the dates in order. (Remember: **B.C.** before **A.D.** and **B.C.** dates go "backwards.") Write each date by an architectural style starting from the earliest to the latest date.

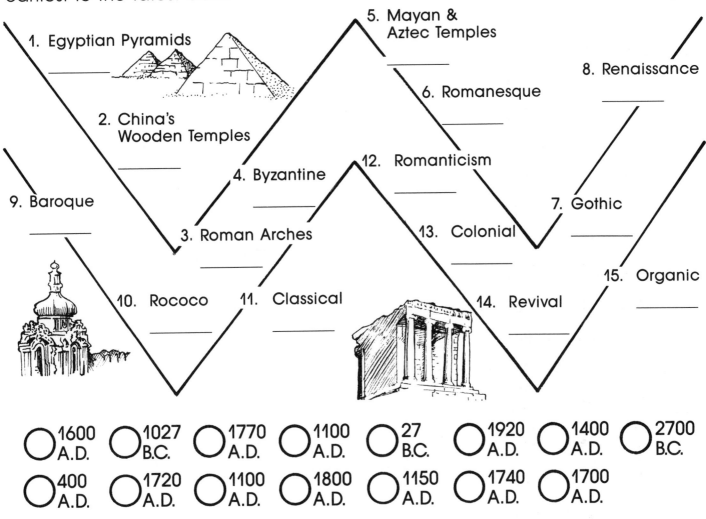

1. Egyptian Pyramids

2. China's Wooden Temples _____

9. Baroque _____

4. Byzantine _____

3. Roman Arches _____

5. Mayan & Aztec Temples _____

6. Romanesque _____

8. Renaissance _____

12. Romanticism _____

13. Colonial _____

7. Gothic _____

15. Organic _____

10. Rococo _____

11. Classical

14. Revival _____

○ 1600 A.D. ○ 1027 B.C. ○ 1770 A.D. ○ 1100 A.D. ○ 27 B.C. ○ 1920 A.D. ○ 1400 A.D. ○ 2700 B.C.

○ 400 A.D. ○ 1720 A.D. ○ 1100 A.D. ○ 1800 A.D. ○ 1150 A.D. ○ 1740 A.D. ○ 1700 A.D.

Write **before** or **after** on each line.

The Baroque Period came _____ the Byzantine Period.

The Revival Period came _____ the Rococo Period.

The Period of Mayan and Aztec temples came _____ the Gothic Period.

The Classical Period came _____ the Renaissance Period.

The Period of Egyptian pyramids came _____ the Organic Period.

The Romanesque Period came _____ the Colonial Period.

The Period of China's Wooden Temples came _____ the Period of Roman Arches.

 IF8712 Reading Skills

Sequencing

Probably the most popular form of entertainment, TV is a mystery to most people. Read the following paragraph which tells how a color TV works.

Color TV begins with a TV camera. A mirror separates the light from a scene into red, blue and green. A microphone changes sounds into audio signals. Camera tubes change the color light into video signals. These signals go to an encoder which makes a new color signal. A transmitter combines the audio and video signals for broadcast.

A receiver picks up the signals with an antenna. The signals move to the tuner which selects the correct station. The signals are separated into audio and video signals. The audio signals are changed into sound. The video signals are changed back to red, blue and green light. The TV screen is covered with dots of red, blue and green. The dots glow and form a color picture.

Write **1 – 13** to put the sentences in the correct order.

◯ The signals move to the tuner which selects the correct station.

◯ A microphone changes sounds into audio signals.

◯ The TV screen is covered with dots of red, blue and green.

◯ The signals go to an encoder which makes a new color signal.

◯ The dots glow and form a color picture.

◯ Color TV begins with a TV camera.

◯ The video signals are changed back to red, blue and green light.

◯ A receiver picks up the signals with an antenna.

◯ The signals are separated into audio and video signals.

◯ Camera tubes change the color light into video signals.

◯ The audio signals are changed into sounds.

◯ A mirror separates the light from a scene into red, blue and green.

◯ A transmitter combines audio and video signals for broadcast.

Vocabulary

Quick Change

The first and last word in each sequence have been given. Change only one letter at a time in the middle steps to reach the final word. Then write each middle step word in the sentence in which it belongs. The sentences are not necessarily in order.

TRACK

— — — — —

— — — — —

— — — — —

CRAVE

The settlers made friends with one Indian _____.

Luke found a piece of wood to act as a _____ for the wobbly cabinet.

There was not a _____ of any foul play in the woman's sudden death.

BLIND

— — — — —

— — — — —

— — — — —

PLANT

The cookies were _____, much to our disappointment.

The men put a _____ from the steps of the new house over the muddy ditch in front of them.

Much to the teacher's surprise, Sandy turned in a

_____ piece of paper.

PORCH

— — — — —

— — — — —

— — — — —

TOUGH

The kangaroo carried the baby in its _____.

After two weeks, Larry went to the doctor for his

_____.

The dog jumped up on the family's new _____ with a bone.

TOWEL

— — — — —

— — — — —

— — — — —

JOKER

After the storm was over, it took the _____ company several hours to fix the lights.

The ranger had to leave the _____ when the flames came close.

Dad used a _____ to stoke the fire.

Vocabulary

Fill in the blanks with a word from the box to the left of each group.

YARD
MINUTE
AUTONOMOUS
SCRIPT
LESS
QUILL
CORE
YELLOW
NUMERALS
FLAME
UNIVERSE

_____ is to play as choreography is to dance. Fence is to _____ as border is to state. _____ is to stench as porcupine is to skunk. Aquarius is to Zodiac as Venus is to _____. _____ is to gregarious as single is to many. Flake is to _____ as chasm is to charm. Grand is to voluminous as petite is to _____. Prefix is to suffix as anti is to _____. Letters are to words as _____ are to numbers. _____ is to earth as eye is to hurricane. Red is to Ned as _____ is to fellow.

PARAGRAPHS
PLANT
BOTANIST
ORAL
FINISH
SAILOR
DISTANCE
SCENT
CANVAS
BARE
STATE

Vocabulary is to paragraph as _____ are to books. Aural is to hearing as _____ is to speaking. _____ is to bear as beat is to beet. Pen is to paper as brush is to _____. Zoologist is to _____ as ape is to coleus. Soldier is to army as _____ is to navy. Time is to _____ as hour is to mile. Quilt is to sew as _____ is to sow. Exam is to final as end is to _____. _____ is to odor as cent is to money. County is to _____ as state is to nation.

Vocabulary   Name _____

Circle the answers within the following questions.

Would you use a lariat for a trip on the river or a cow on the range?

Would a person who is subtle be delicate and cunning or boistrous and wild?

Would a patina be an old finish or a little bear?

Would a breach be a place to swim or a break of contract?

Would you use a thesaurus to look for synonyms or definitions of words?

Would a choreographer map out the coral reefs on the ocean floor or the steps of a dance on the stage?

Would cholesterol be found in chicken eggs or in a diamond mine?

Would a faction be a partial whole number or a sub-group sharing like beliefs?

Would you placate a person to calm him down or prepare him for surgery?

Would you see a philatelist at a stamp show or an outdoor show?

Would a frugal person be apt to have the first dollar ever earned or a tendency to get sick often?

Would you use a calaboose to detain a criminal or store fodder for pigs?

Would an aptitude test determine one's ability or agility?

Would a cartographer be knowledgeable about meridians and parallels or carts, cars and carriages?

Would a biased person be one who has a prejudice or no money?

Would you use calipers when measuring the distance between fence posts or the thickness of a pipe?

Would you masticate your dinner or your dog?

Would you extricate a criminal for trial or a tooth for filling?

Would a deplorable person cheat his best friend or study diplomacy?

Would you incarcerate a pig for market or a man for breaking the law?

Would you be apt to see a menagerie at a circus or a courthouse?

Would a tenacious person be prone to tendonitis or stubbornness?

Would you use a scythe to comb your hair or cut the weeds?

Would a neurologist care for you or study neutrons?

Using Is Confusing!

Above each pair of sentences are two or three words. Write the correct word in each sentence.

lying　laying　lying

I am _____ the book on the table.

I am _____ about who took the book to protect him.

I am _____ down for awhile.

beside　besides

Our cat was buried _____ our dog in the backyard.

_____ making dessert for the church social, Mary made salad.

uninterested　disinterested

They chose a _____ person to act as the referee to settle the argument.

The _____ man was bored when he had to go to the ballet with his wife.

inflammable　inflammatory

Tempers flared after the _____ speech.

Be careful to select _____ material when knitting the baby's sweater.

lay　laid　lied

I _____ down yesterday for a little while.

I _____ yesterday when I said I would go with you.

I _____ the ornament carefully on the shelf.

biennially　biannually

Congressmen from every state are elected _____ to the House of Representatives in Washington.

The Science Club meets _____,March first and September first, to share their findings.

amend　emend

They had to _____ the lease by adding a clause about damage.

Before Terry typed his report, he had to _____ it where necessary.

Vocabulary

Name _____

 **What's What?**

Above each pair of sentences are two words written with their diacritical spellings. Write the regular spelling for the two words on the line to the right of them. Then, use the diacritical spelling to write the correct word in each sentence.

proj´ ekt   prō jekt´   _____

The speaker needs to _____ his voice.

The Garden Club agreed to make beautifying the city their _____ for the year.

pra dōōs´   prō´ doos   _____

The _____ at the market was spoiled.

Jim and Jerry wanted to _____ a play for the class.

wōōnd   wound   _____

The nurse bandaged Tim's _____.

Larry _____ the string around the gate to hold it shut.

kan tent´   kon´ tent   _____

The boys were disappointed to find the box's _____ was nothing but broken glass.

The boys were _____ to stay inside and watch television when it started to rain.

min´ it   mī nōōt´   _____

There was a _____ piece of dirt on the camera lens.

In just a _____ the bell will ring for third period.

in val´ ad   in´ va lid   _____

The results of the race were _____ because the timer started his watch late.
The results of the medical tests showed that Gramps would soon be an

_____.

wīnd   wind   _____

Debris flew everywhere when the _____ kicked up.

Hank forgot to _____ his alarm, and so he was late for work.

Name _____

Brains Speak!

Begin where the arrow is pointing. Decode the message clockwise in each brain. Then write a reply from the "speaker's" mouth.

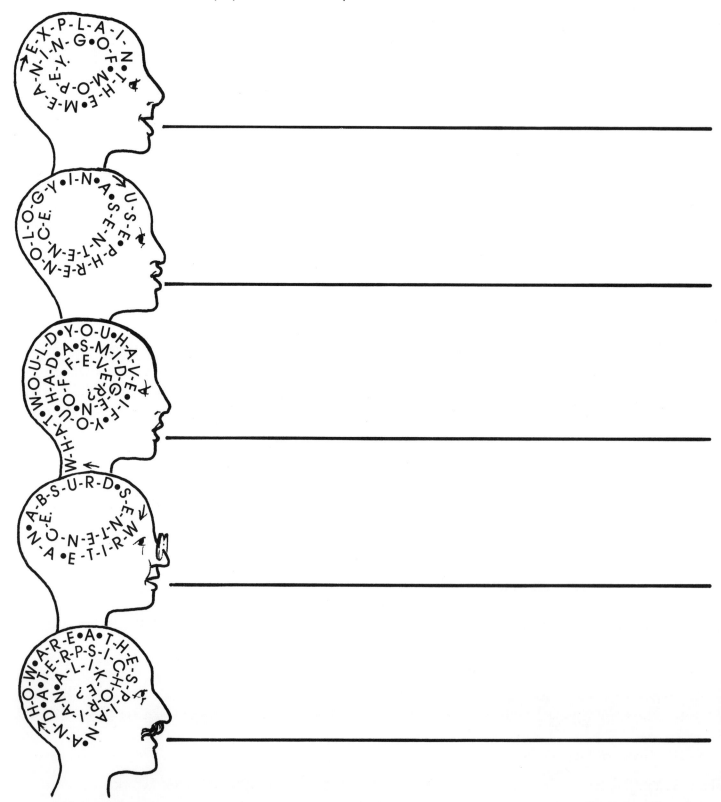

Vocabulary

Name _____

There's Truth to This!

Color the conjunctions yellow, the prepositions blue and the adverbs green.
Find a message about you.

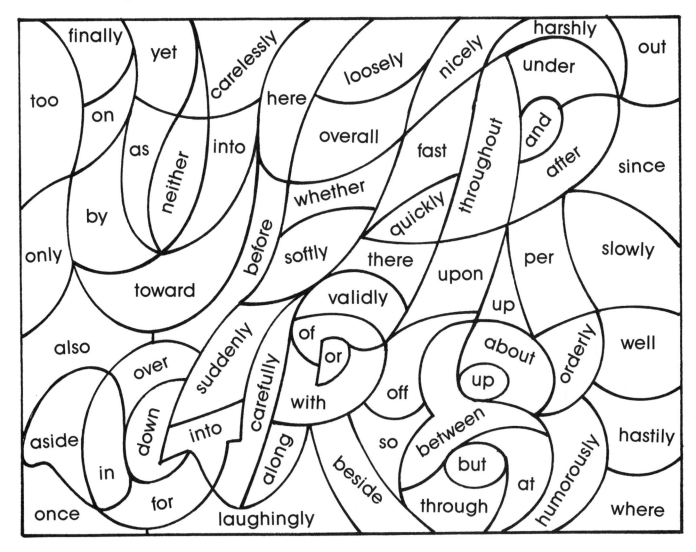

Write one sentence using one of the conjunctions.

_____

Write two sentences using one of the prepositions above in each sentence.

_____

_____

Write two sentences using one of the adverbs above in each sentence.

_____

Vocabulary   Name _____

Unscramble the adjectives below.

hiteg ___eight___   ilaeg _____

ilvjoa _____   glines _____

ourasougec _____   lemwol _____

edergy _____   kicdew _____

udends _____   nanaul _____

cenedt _____   velloy _____

nugoy _____   lnamyren _____

itctatarve _____   gridif _____

Unscramble the adverbs below.

bofree _____   fyeblauulti _____

tanyle _____   sisbeed _____

veabo _____   woeritshe _____

oorlyhguht _____   tlasom _____

tyslfo _____   sdmoel _____

yislae _____   rlyrdhuei _____

taleuyi _____   sslyineb _____

cehwne _____   lgneyt _____

Use a word from above that will make sense in the sentences below.

Jason acted _____ when he lost his _____ house key.

Wendy saw the _____ team _____ they lost the _____ game.

The cookies were hidden _____ the refrigerator.

_____ _____ racers ran into each other when they hit a bump.

Everyone _____ enjoyed the movie.

Frank _____ turns his work in on time.

When you pet a newborn pet, handle it _____.

Who else is going _____ the three boys?

They _____ cut the grass so they could play ball.

The _____ music was playing _____.

Vocabulary

 **Next of Kin**

Name _____

Circle two or three of the words in parentheses which are related in some way to the word on the left.

kin   (ancestors   relatives   descendents   ascends   friend)
flower   (rapid   petal   tall   pedal   stem)
barrel   (race   final   stave   witch   rainwater)
finances   (account   school   spirit   weather   taxes)
medical   (linotype   scalpel   sutures   prescription   marble)
performer   (roll   theater   script   companion   role)
compass   (plate   direction   needle   spider   quantity)
bone   (calcium   harmful   tibia   phonetic   vegetation)
desert   (forest   sandy   arid   zebras   equator)
instrument   (microscope   chorus   calliope   surgeon   axe)
infant   (toddler   carriage   lullaby   chemical   longitude)
tackle   (reel   football   bridle   ocean   psychotic)
equipment   (manpower   paraphernalia   vintage   accoutrement)
tripod   (telescope   photography   transit   tricycle   peas)
religious   (pious   cathedral   sensitive   fastidious   alter)
military   (platoon   maneuvers   armory   dresser   prison)

Use some of the circled words from above to complete the sentences below.

1. Milk has a lot of _____ in it.

2. The pharmacist filled the _____ quickly.

3. Every Saturday the _____ serves as a center for the military.

4. The climate was hot and _____.

5. He packed all the _____ necessary to do the job.

6. The _____ wavered three degrees.

7. The preacher was a _____ man.

8. The surveyor set up his _____ to prepare for the new highway.

9. The _____ was warped.

10. When the merry-go-round went around, the _____ played.

11. The director of the drama interpreted the _____ for the actors.

Thinking Skills

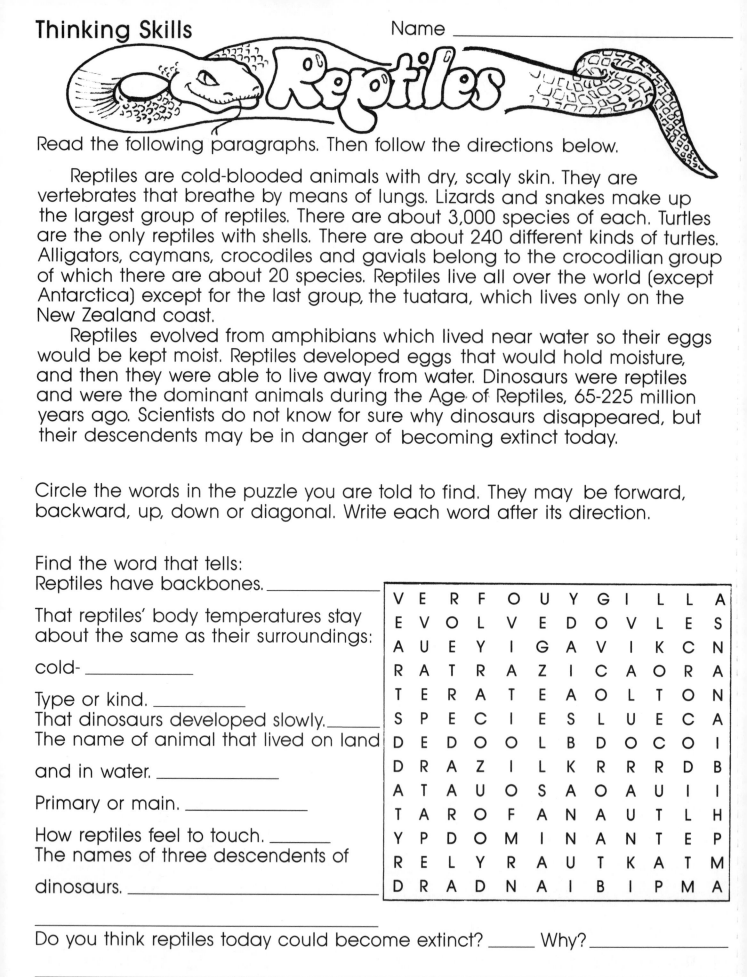

Name _____

Read the following paragraphs. Then follow the directions below.

Reptiles are cold-blooded animals with dry, scaly skin. They are vertebrates that breathe by means of lungs. Lizards and snakes make up the largest group of reptiles. There are about 3,000 species of each. Turtles are the only reptiles with shells. There are about 240 different kinds of turtles. Alligators, caymans, crocodiles and gavials belong to the crocodilian group of which there are about 20 species. Reptiles live all over the world (except Antarctica) except for the last group, the tuatara, which lives only on the New Zealand coast.

Reptiles evolved from amphibians which lived near water so their eggs would be kept moist. Reptiles developed eggs that would hold moisture, and then they were able to live away from water. Dinosaurs were reptiles and were the dominant animals during the Age of Reptiles, 65-225 million years ago. Scientists do not know for sure why dinosaurs disappeared, but their descendents may be in danger of becoming extinct today.

Circle the words in the puzzle you are told to find. They may be forward, backward, up, down or diagonal. Write each word after its direction.

Find the word that tells:
Reptiles have backbones. _____

That reptiles' body temperatures stay about the same as their surroundings:

cold- _____

Type or kind. _____
That dinosaurs developed slowly. _____
The name of animal that lived on land

and in water. _____

Primary or main. _____

How reptiles feel to touch. _____
The names of three descendents of

dinosaurs. _____

V	E	R	F	O	U	Y	G	I	L	L	A
E	V	O	L	V	E	D	O	V	L	E	S
A	U	E	Y	I	G	A	V	I	K	C	N
R	A	T	R	A	Z	I	C	A	O	R	A
T	E	R	A	T	E	A	O	L	T	O	N
S	P	E	C	I	E	S	L	U	E	C	A
D	E	D	O	O	L	B	D	O	C	O	I
D	R	A	Z	I	L	K	R	R	R	D	B
A	T	A	U	O	S	A	O	A	U	I	I
T	A	R	O	F	A	N	A	U	T	L	H
Y	P	D	O	M	I	N	A	N	T	E	P
R	E	L	Y	R	A	U	T	K	A	T	M
D	R	A	D	N	A	I	B	I	P	M	A

_____

Do you think reptiles today could become extinct? _____ Why? _____

_____

Name _____

Natural Resources

The dwindling supply of some of America's resources has led concerned environmentalists to call for the recycling of wastes. Recycling is the process of recovering used materials, separating them from non-usable wastes, and sending them to manufacturers who make them into usable products. There are many recycling centers throughout the country. Often scouts or school programs have campaigns to gather waste materials.

Most common among recycled wastes are newspapers, aluminum and steel cans, and glass bottles. They provide material for several usable products and, at the same time, save our natural resources.

Paper comes from trees. Containers are made from minerals from the earth. Not only do manufacturers use up natural resources when they lumber or mine for these products, but they add to environmental pollution.

What natural resources are being conserved with recycling?_____

_____

What could happen to animal and plant life if all natural resources

disappeared? _____

_____

What might non-usable wastes be?_____

Of what help is recycling? _____

_____

What products might waste materials become? _____

Which Path to Take?

Explain the two paths a tree could take, which you think is the better and

why? _____

_____

See the Poes Grow!

Mr. and Mrs. Poe had five children. They kept a growing chart for each child from birth to age twelve. Read the graph below and answer the questions beneath it.

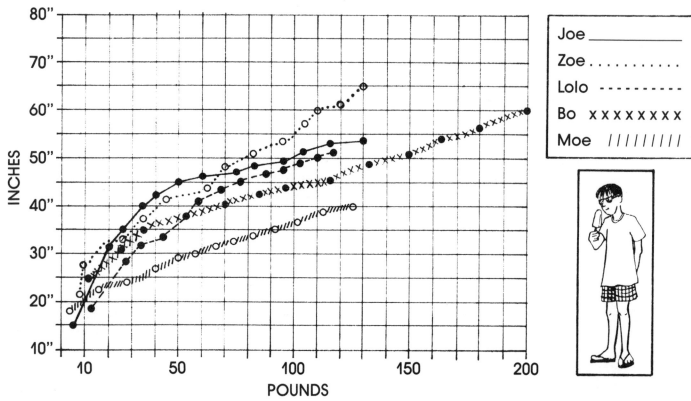

Joe _____
Zoe . . . .
Lolo - - - - - - - -
Bo x x x x x x x x
Moe / / / / / / / / /

Who was born the shortest? _____ tallest? _____

Who was born the heaviest? _____ lightest? _____

Who was the shortest at age 12? _____ tallest? _____

Who was the heaviest at age 12? _____ lightest? _____

How tall was Lolo at age 8? _____

How much did Moe weight at age 3? _____

How many inches did Zoe grow from birth to age 12? _____

How many pounds did Zoe gain from age 9 to age 12? _____

Label their pictures taken at age 12.

Write a **T** in front of each statement below if it is true.
Write an **F** in front of each statement below if it is fantasy. If you are in doubt, look the subject up. When you have finished marking the statements, color the numbers of the TRUE statements in the puzzle below red, and the numbers of the FANTASY statements orange to make a fantasy picture.

____ 1. Dr. Doolittle took care of the animals.
____ 2. Women thought to be witches were persecuted in America's early settlement days.
____ 3. Harry Houdini was an escape artist who could free himself from a nailed crate.
____ 4. John Henry was a steel-driving man who died with a hammer in his hand.
____ 5. A unicorn is a horse with a horn.
____ 6. The teddy bear was named for President T. R. Roosevelt after he refused to shoot a baby cub.
____ 7. Mike Fink was the greatest riverman on the Mississippi.
____ 8. Pecos Bill was a cowboy who invented many cowboy skills and was the first to throw a lariat.
____ 9. Tom Sawyer got all his friends to paint his fence.
____ 10. Trees usually blossom before they bear fruit.
____ 11. George Washington chopped down a cherry tree and could not tell a lie.
____ 12. Orion was a great Greek hunter.
____ 13. Snoopy is a human-acting beagle that hangs around with Lucy and Charlie Brown.
____ 14. The boll weevil is a beetle that feeds on cotton plants.
____ 15. Davy Crockett was a famous frontiersman.
____ 16. Dorothy traveled down the yellow brick road.
____ 17. Laika, a Russian dog, was the first animal to orbit Earth.
____ 18. Johnny Appleseed gave apple seeds away to early American settlers.

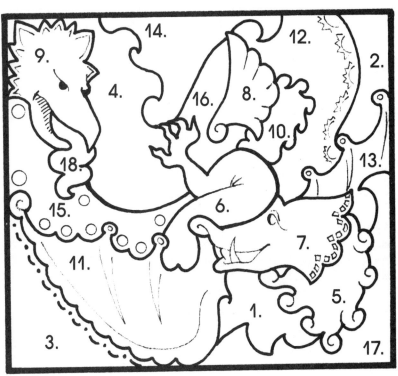

Name _____

Look at the "comic strips" below. Each one tells an incomplete story. Complete it in the last box of each strip. Then, below the strip, write an ending for the story.

_____

_____

_____

_____

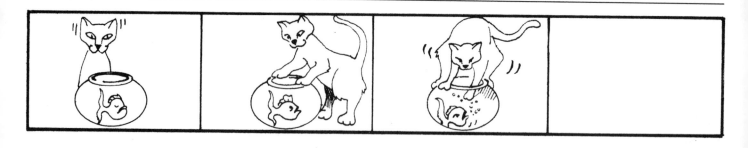

_____

_____

_____

_____

Thinking Skills

Who or What Am I?

Write what each paragraph is describing under it (1) and what clue gave it away (2). You can find the answers in the puzzle below. The answers appear in a running order, but not necessarily in a straight line. They may run up or down, back and forth or criss-cross. See the example to the right.

```
   3.
1. D   O   M   H
2. F   G   R   C
   A   E   R   E
   T   H   Y   C  4.
```

1. dog
2. father
3. mice
4. cry

I was once the political head of a country. I helped lead my country to victory in World War II. I met with Stalin and Roosevelt.

1. I am _____.

2. _____

I am a state. My climate is usually dry. I have mountains and deserts. I was one of the last four states admitted to the Union. The first capital of the U.S. was located in me under Spanish rule.

1. I am _____.

2. _____

As early as the 1400 and 1500's, some of my countrymen walked on U.S. land. They traveled a long way to get there. I am on the Iberian peninsula. My western and southern borders are on the Atlantic Ocean. Spain borders me to the north and east.

1. I am _____.

2. _____

I like to swim. I have lungs and must come to the surface sometimes to breathe. I am a mammal and give birth to live young. The tail of a fish is vertical. Mine is horizontal.

1. I am a _____.

2. _____

I was President of the U.S. I ran for the presidency but was defeated. I lost to Jimmy Carter.

1. I am _____.

2. _____

I have to study a long time to do what I do. I am especially good at drawing and arithmetic. People come to me to design new products and structures. I look for better ways of using existing resources and developing new materials.

1. I am an _____.

2. _____

I can live a long time if conditions are right. I am the oldest known living thing. I am the largest of all plants.

1. I am a _____.

2. _____

```
I   W   O   I   G   E   L   H   A   E   R   A
N   X   C   N   N   L   W   L   L   G   L   D
S   E   I   E   E   E   I   E   T   A   E   F
T   N   M   W   N   R   H   P   R   E   G   O
O   C   H   U   R   C   O   R   T   U   R   D
```

Name _____

_____

Read the following paragraphs and answer the questions after them.

    In 1821, William Becknell led the first wagon train from Franklin, Missouri, to Santa Fe, New Mexico. It was not easy. This was the beginning of a trade route, called the Santa Fe Trail, that was to last for fifty years.

    The only outsiders the Indians of the West had known until the start of the trail had been the Spanish. The Indians had learned about horses and metal from the Spanish. The relations between the two were not always friendly, but the Indians liked some of their goods and adapted them to their lifestyle. When the wagon trains began crossing the prairies, the relationship between the Indians and the "Easterners" was somewhat the same. Some welcomed the goods being brought for trade. Some felt the arrival of the wagon trains was an invasion of their lands.

    Forts were built along the Trail to protect the growing trade and passenger route and the many men who were brought to build the railroad. Soon after the railroad began service, the Santa Fe Trail ceased to operate.

Name three hardships you think the people on the wagon trains may have encountered.

_____

_____

What do you think some of the goods were that the wagon trains carried west? _____

With what goods do you think the wagon trains returned to the east? _____

_____

After the railroad was in operation, would you have traveled west on the Santa Fe Trail or on the train? _____ Why? _____

_____

Why do you think the Santa Fe Trail stopped operating? _____

_____

Write a title for this article above it on the line at the top of the page.

Hats, Etc.

First read the article about "Hats, Etc." without filling in any of the blanks.
Read it again. Think about what word would make sense in each blank.
Select a word from the box beneath the article. Write it where it belongs.

A hat is the _____ given to a piece ___ clothing worn on the head. ___ hat has a crown _____ a _____. Other head _____ such as hoods, bonnets, and caps have no _____, but will be considered _____ in this article.

People wear hats for _____ reasons. One is _____ protection. They may protect the wearer _____ the climate or from bodily injury. Cowboys _____ hats to keep cool and _____ players wear helmets to _____ from injuring themselves. Some _____ of headgear signal the _____ profession or position. A _____ from high school wears a _____ with a tassel. ___ Eskimo's hood tells he _____ from a cold climate. The _____ worker's helmet signals his _____ of work. The third _____ for wearing a hat ___ appearance. Ladies like to _____ themselves attractive. Men may wear hats _____ business appointments.

No one knows exactly _____ or why hats developed, but _____ have been a part of _____ culture for millions of years.

A	form	brim	name	from	coverings	graduate	and
football	forms	cap	type	make	wearer's	An	how
they	for	our		is	to	reason	of	hats
different	comes	construction		wear	keep		

Tell who might wear the hats below and why.

_____ _____ _____ _____

_____ _____ _____ _____

_____ _____ _____ _____

Name _____

Prehistoric Transportation

First read the article about "Prehistoric Transportation" without filling in any of the blanks. Read it again. This time, think about what letters would fit in the blanks and make sense. Write them in where they belong.

Prehistoric times probably were from about 5,000,000 years ago until around 3000 B.C. Transportation, as we think of it, probably did not begin until around 10,000 B.C.

In the beginning, there were not domesti__ated animals, w__eels or roads. People w__lked. When they t__aveled, everyth__ng they wanted t__ carry was s__rapped onto their bodie__. If it was too heavy, it was strapped to a pole and two people __ __rried the pole. F__om __hi__ developed __he sledge which could be __ttached to a person and dra__g__d along the ground be__ind the pers__n. __unner__ w__re a__ded to the sledge in late p__ehistoric times.

By __bout 8000 B.C., the donkey and ox __ere domesticated a__d were u__ed for farm work. Be__ween 3000-4500 years late__, th__ animals w__re used as pack animals and harnesses were inven__ed so the animals __ould pull sledges __s humans had done befo__e them. Animal__ could tr__nsport heav__e__ load__.

Wit__ the format__on of communities, the need for better trans__ortation developed. Raft__, dugou__s and cano__s were invented __round this ti__e for use on inland s__ __eams and l__kes. Oars and poles were used to move them __ __ w__ter.

The f__ __st vehic__es w__th wheels were inve__t__d in Mesopotamia a__ound 3500 B.C. The Egyptians invented s__ilboats aro__nd 3200 B.C. Wi__h these inventi__n__, transportation developed eventually to what we know today.

Write the letters used as fill-ins above in order to spell the names of eight vehicles that developed throughout time. Write the names below. (Some vehicles are more than one word.)

_____

_____

Thinking Skills

Name _____

What's For Sure?

Write an **F** in front of each statement below if it is a fact.
Write an **O** in front of each statement if it is an opinion.

____ 1. Fel(i)x Mendelssohn(f)irst played the piano in public when he was ten.

____ 2. The Republicans in Congress usuall(y) are better politicians than the Dem(o)crats.

____ 3. Dwight Goodin is tho(u)ght to be one of baseball's finest players.

____ 4. Rhode Island was the thirteenth state(i)n 1790.

____ 5. Many people think the Presi(d)ent is doing a good job.

____ 6. Marsupials are mammals tha(t) give birth to underdeveloped young.

____ 7. Food cooked in tinfoil may not b(e) healthy.

____ 8. Cyrus McCormick (i)nvented (t)he reaper.

____ 9. Labor Day is always observed on the f(i)rst Monday of (S)eptember.

____ 10. Rock mu(s)ic has a strong b(e)at and is usually loud.

____ 11. Abraham Lincoln was (a)ssassinated at Ford's Theater.

____ 12. Tige(r)s are like little kittens; they are so cute.

____ 13. Queen Victoria ruled England longer (t)han any other monarch.

____ 14. There are more (D)emocrats in the House of Representatives than Republicans.

____ 15. The opera, "Porgy and Bess," is the best American opera e(v)er writt(e)n.

____ 16. Robert Da(w)son has written many books for young readers.

____ 17. H(a)waii is the most beautiful of all the states.

____ 18. New York Cit(y) has the largest p(o)pulation of all American cities.

____ 19. The Amazon River is the longest river in the world.

____ 20. The blossom(s) seem (t)o be later this ye(a)r than last yea(r).

____ 21. The land west of the Mississippi River covers a gre(a)ter area, but has fewer people living in it, than the area of land ea(s)t of the Mississippi in the United States.

____ 22. It is n(o)t safe to fix wires in an electrical appliance while it is still plugged into a live so(c)ket.

The circled letters in the opinion statements spell out a fact about you. What is it? (4 words) _____

He Likes Me, He Likes Me Not!

Below are several sets of likes and dislikes. Figure out what it is in each set that makes the first part likeable and the second part not. After each set, write what the difference is between the likes and dislikes.

Mary likes cardinals, but she does not like blue jays.
Mary likes tomatoes, but she does not like squash.
Mary likes blood, but she does not like saliva.
Mary likes strawberries, but she does not like boysenberries.

_____

Harry likes a drum, but he does not like a clarinet.
Harry likes basketballs, but he does not like footballs.
Harry likes pennies, but he does not like dollars.
Harry likes to ride a ferris wheel, but he does not like to ride a roller coaster.

_____

Gayle likes marching bands, but she does not like rubber bands.
Gayle likes flashy cars, but she does not like pickup trucks.
Gayle likes to play darts, but she does not like to play pool.
Gayle likes a warm dinner, but she does not like hot drinks.

_____

Babies like beards, but they do not like eyeglasses.
Babies like monkeys, but they do not like penguins.
Babies like gerbils, but they do not like whales.
Babies like tarantulas, but they do not like roaches.

_____

Everyone likes George, but no one likes Gary.
Everyone likes Robert, but no one likes Richard.
Everyone likes Jeanne, not no one likes Janet.
Everyone likes Merideth, but no one likes Martha.

_____

Now make up a like-dislike set of your own. See if a friend or your teacher can figure it out.

_____
_____
_____
_____
_____

Thinking Skills

Read the following article and answer the questions below.

Marble is a type of metamorphic rock formed from limestone. This type of rock was formed millions of years ago. Heat and pressure in the Earth's crust caused the limestone to undergo changes. This process is called recrystallization.

Impurities in the limestone, plus the temperature at the time of the crystallization, affected the mineral composition of the marble. A greater quantity of quartz resulted when the temperature was low. At higher temperatures, rarer minerals may have been produced. At times when all impurities reacted together, garnet, a precious stone, may have been formed in the marble.

The presence of minerals in greater or lesser amounts is what gives marble its color. The purest calcite marble is white. Hematite gives marble a reddish color. Marble with limonite is yellow, and marble with serpentine is green.

Marble is found in many places around the world. Georgia mines more marble than any other state. It is a strong rock that polishes well and resists weathering. It is very difficult to mine.

1. For what do you think marble is used? _____
   _____

2. Why do you think it is used for these purposes? _____
   _____

3. Do you think marble formed at high or low temperatures is more valuable?
   _____ Why? _____
   _____

4. From what natural resource does marble come? _____

5. Following are some well-known structures made of marble. Unscramble the

   letters to find out what they are.

   nasiWnthgo tmMneout _____

   naroPetnh _____   gWneid riVcyto _____

   niLnloc loieaMrm _____

   ajT aahlM _____   enngiLa wrToe fo iPas _____

Name _____

If You Were Asked...

If you were asked or told to do the following, tell what would be the first thing you would do or ask?

1. Prepare meat loaf for dinner._____

2. Take the dog for a walk._____

3. Go to the store for mother. _____

4. Write a report about weather in Chile._____

5. To be at school by 7:30 _____

6. Come home alone after school. _____

7. Call a taxi. _____

8. Get ready to go to a party._____

9. Shelve books for the librarian._____

10. To be a patrol person _____

11. R.S.V.P. _____

12. Fix a leaky faucet. _____

13. Prepare lettuce for a salad._____

14. Sign for a C.O.D. package. _____

15. Baby-sit a neighbor's child. _____

16. Plan a trip to _____.(Name it.)_____

17. To go to a friend's after school _____

18. Earn some money._____

19. Use a pay phone. _____

20. Plan a camping trip._____

21. Walk in the dark through the woods._____

22. Save money. _____

23. Take attendance._____

24. Help a friend find a lost wallet._____

25. Conserve energy._____

26. Respond to a cry of "Help!" _____

27. Buy a present for a friend._____

28. Cut material to make a tablecloth._____

Name _____

Give Them a Name!

Read each paragraph below. Give each one a title on the line above it.

_____

Lacrosse was first played by American Indians. It is a game played with a ball and a stick that has a net pocket at one end. The object of the game is to score goals by throwing or kicking the ball into the opposing team's goal.

_____

Marble players have their own vocabulary. Players who shoot marbles use a "shooter" to score points by hitting "object" marbles. Usually when they shoot, players "knuckle down." Some kinds of marbles have slang names such as "glassies" and "steelies."

_____

Horses used in the game of polo are called polo ponies. They are small as one might think when hearing the word "pony." Polo ponies must be fast and strong and must get used to clubs swinging overhead and being bumped by other horses upon their rider's commands. Training a pony is hard work and takes about a year.

_____

Hundreds of games can be played with cards. Solitaire is played alone. Fish and Hearts can be played with two or more players. Poker can be played with as many as ten.

_____

There are many kinds of contests of speed. Dog racing has been a sport since ancient times. Horses compete in trotting, pacing and running races. Automobile racing has occurred almost since the first car rolled off the assembly line. Boating, swimming and flying are some other racing forms.

_____

Besides the bats and balls used in a baseball game, each player has his own equipment. Every player wears a uniform with a number on it, shoes with spikes and has his own glove. The catcher has a special glove plus a mask, chest protector and shin guards.

_____

Jacks, as we know it today, is a game often played by children using ten metal objects with six points and a ball. The game probably came from "pebble Jacks," a game still played in Europe and Asia. A similar, and even older, game originated in Asia using the knucklebones of small animals.

_____

Pieces used in chess are called: Pawn, Knight, Bishop, Rook, Queen and King. Rules govern their moves. The pieces, also called men, may be assigned different values according to their position and relation to other men during a game.

What do all these paragraphs have in common? _____

Name _____

Guess What?

Look at each square. A part of something is showing. Write what you think it is below each square.

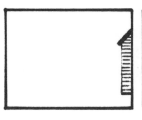  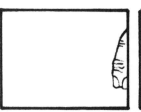  

  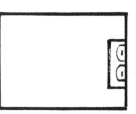 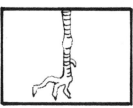 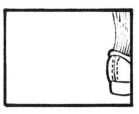

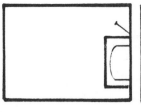    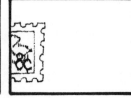

 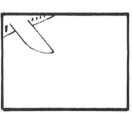 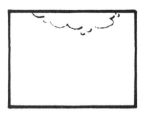  

   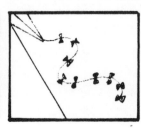 

Thinking Skills

Name _____

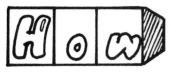 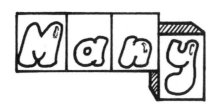 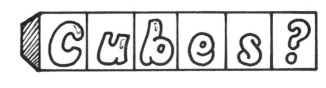

Each figure below is made of more than one cube.
A single cube would look like this.
Look at the figures below. Determine how many cubes comprise each figure.
Write your answer in the triangle by each one.

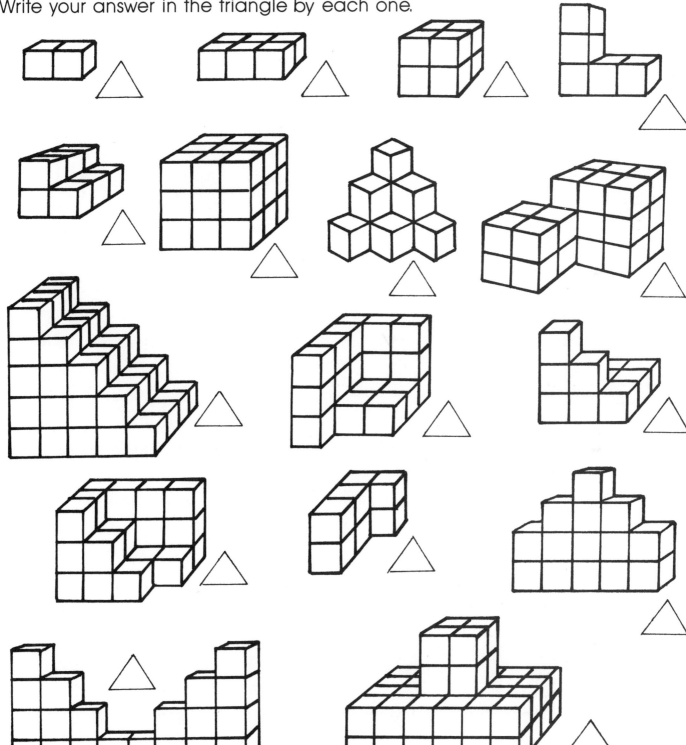

Thinking Skills

Name _____

Measure Up!

Look at each graph. Fill in the blanks in the sentences with the correct words, names or numbers.

6th Grade Girls

Tanya is ___ feet ___ inches tall. She is shorter than Sally and _____. Marty is the _____ by _____ inches. _____ is one inch shorter than _____.

_____ and _____ are the same height.

Holly is _____ inches _____ than Sally and Debbie, who are ___ inches _____ than _____.

What is this graph measuring? _____

Write the girls' names from shortest to tallest.

_____

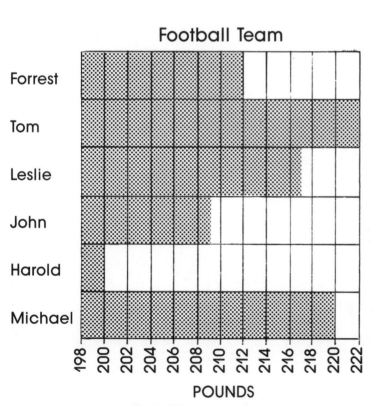

Football Team

_____ weighs ___ _____ less than Forrest.

_____ _____ _____ pounds less than _____, the _____ player on the team.

_____ weighs halfway between the weights of Tom and _____.

Although Harold is _____ than Tom by _____ pounds, he is tough.

_____ _____ almost as much as the heaviest player, but he is not strong.

What is the graph measuring? _____

Write the boys' names from the heaviest to the lightest. _____

_____

Answer Key

Page 1

Following Directions   Name _____

🎵 Compose a Name! 🎵

Follow the directions to learn the name of a composer.

Direction	Answer
Start with a word that is used to light a fire.	match
Add a word that means a short rest.	matchnap
Drop the word that means an adult male.	tchap
Add a word that is a form of precipitation.	tchaprain
Add a word that could mean the smallest living thing in your body or a small "room" in a jail.	tchapraincell
Drop the word that describes the step of a high-stepping horse.	tchaill
Add a word that names a bird that "coos".	tchailldove
Drop the double consonant.	tchaidove
Drop the fourth letter of the alphabet. Replace it with the eleventh letter.	tchaikove
Add the word that contains the sun, stars, etc.	tchaikovesky
Drop the fourth vowel in this word and you will have the last name of this composer.	Tchaikovsky

Now learn the name of a ballet he wrote (two words).

Direction	Answer
Write the name of a prickly plant. (It begins with th.)	thistle
Add a word that means neat.	thistleneat
Drop the word that means skinny.	stleeat
Add the name of an evergreen tree that begins with p.	stleeatpine
Drop the two consonants that are the same.	sleeapine
Replace the final letter of the word with the seventh letter of the alphabet.	sleeaping
Drop the first letter of the alphabet.	sleeping
Add the word that can mean whip or win.	sleeping beat
Add a word that means to destroy or demolish.	sleepingbeatruin
Drop the word for a kind of can.	sleeping bearu
Add the name of a spinning toy.	sleeping bearutop
Add a word that is the opposite of no.	sleeping bearutopyes
Drop the plural word for something used to tie with.	sleepingbeauty
Write the name of the ballet.	Sleeping Beauty

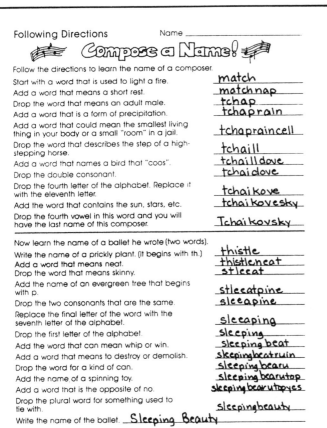

Page 1

Page 2

Following Directions   Name _____

Stomp Man

Make a dot (•) for each of the following points in order. Connect each point as you make it with the previous one.

1. B,4   6. L,18   11. Q,16   16. V,20   21. U,13   26. W,10   31. T,6   36. R,10
2. B,8   7. M,20   12. O,12   17. U,21   22. Y,12   27. U,8   32. U,7   37. M,10
3. H,8   8. O,21   13. R,12   18. S,16   23. Y,11   28. U,10   33. U,4   38. H,6
4. K,11   9. O,19   14. R,16   19. T,11   24. X,11   29. T,10   34. T,5   39. C,7
5. O,16   10. M,18   15. V,24   20. U,11   25. X,10   30. Q,7   35. P,7   40. B,4

Write a set of points (pairs of numbers) that will show what "Stomp Man" is about to crush. Give your set of points to a classmate to solve. ➝

SET OF POINTS

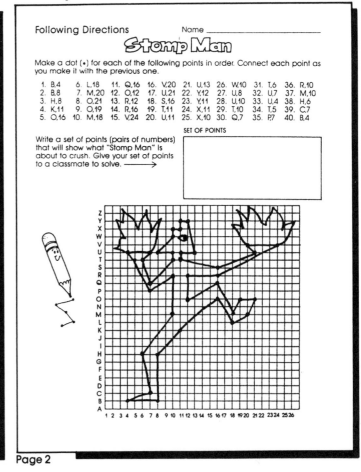

Page 2

Page 3

Following Directions   Name _____

Whose House?

Draw as you are directed.

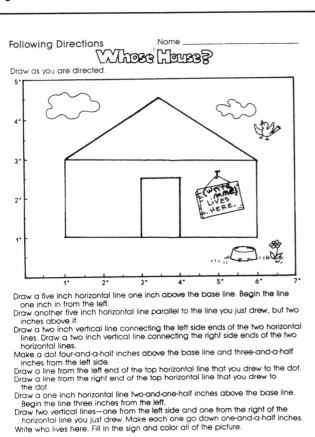

Draw a five inch horizontal line one inch above the base line. Begin the line one inch in from the left.

Draw another five inch horizontal line parallel to the line you just drew, but two inches above it.

Draw a two inch vertical line connecting the left side ends of the two horizontal lines. Draw a two inch vertical line connecting the right side ends of the two horizontal lines.

Make a dot four-and-a-half inches above the base line and three-and-a-half inches from the left side.

Draw a line from the left end of the top horizontal line that you drew to the dot.

Draw a line from the right end of the top horizontal line that you drew to the dot.

Draw a one inch horizontal line two-and-one-half inches above the base line. Begin the line three inches from the left.

Draw two vertical lines—one from the left side and one from the right of the horizontal line you just drew. Make each one go down one-and-a-half inches.

Write who lives here. Fill in the sign and color all of the picture.

Page 3

Page 4

Following Directions   Name _____

Information, Please

When you finish this page, take it home. Keep it in a handy place.

Part One

Write your family name on line 1.
Write your address on line 2.
Write your phone number on line 3.
Write the name and phone number of a friend on line 4.
Write the name and number of your doctor or medical service on line 5.
Write the emergency number for the area where you live on line 6.

1. (family name)
2. (address)
3. (phone number)
4. (friend's + phone #)
5. (doctor's name + number)
6. (emergency number)

Part Two

Use a ruler.
Draw a line from:
A to B
A to C
B to C
E to C
D to F
I to G
H to J
G to M and
H to N
Draw a dotted line from:
C to D
C to G
D to H
G to H
K to L
F to J
M to N and E to I

Part Three

Cut out the figure on the solid lines.
Fold with the written information outward, on the dotted lines.
Put paste on X. Tuck flap X under A-B. Pinch to hold.
Put paste on Y. Tuck flap Y under K-M. Press until it holds.
Put paste on Z. Tuck flap Z under L-N. Press until it holds.

Page 4

Answer Key

Page 5

Following Directions　　Name _____

Alpha Trail

There are many paths through Alpha Park. Every letter you pass equals points. The object is to get through with as few points as possible. The points are as follows:

Add one for every M you pass.
Add two for every F.
Add three for every R.
Subtract one for every V.
Subtract two for every N.

Answers will vary.

Can you find your way through the park under five? Try it.

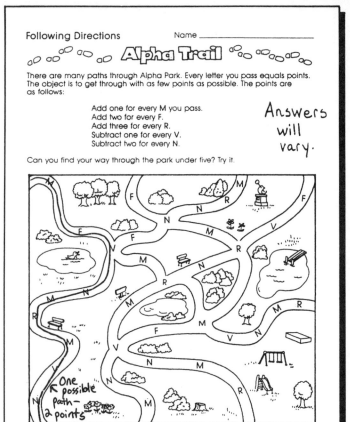

One possible path— 2 points

Page 5

Page 6

Following Directions　　Name _____

Head Over Heels

There are twelve words in this puzzle. Each word starts from the center box and then follows its own path. Find each one by column and/or row number plus its direction. The first one is done as an example.

Example: 1. The first letter, 4E, is 4 spaces to the right (East) of the center box.
4E is C.
The next letter, 2N, is 2 spaces above (North) C. 2N is H.
The third letter, 5W, is 5 spaces to the left (West) of H. 5W is E.
The fourth letter, 3S, is 3 rows below (South) E. 3S is an S.
The last letter, 2W, is 2 columns to the left (West) of S. 2W is T.

Begin the next word from the center and follow its pattern. All the letters will be used and they will only be used once. Cross out each letter as it is used.

I	D	S	H	S	R	D	S	E	R	E
N	L	E	G	E	C	A	E	H	H	M
N	V	H	E	I	S	L	G	R	E	O
E	A	L	A	F	✦	T	H	A	C	F
S	S	T	I	S	S	H	S	E	L	P
E	N	B	A	O	W	S	W	S	D	R
T	B	O	S	I	D	U	N	N	K	O

1. C H E S T
   4E, 2N, 5W, 3S, 2W
2. S H O U L D E R S
   1N, 3W, 4S, 4E, 4N, 2N, 4E, 5S, 4W
3. F I N G E R S
   1W, 3S, 3E, 4N, 2E, 2N, 2W
4. A B D O M E N
   4W, 3S, 4E, 5E, 5N, 3W, 7W
5. F O R E H E A D
   5E, 1N, 2W, 2N, 5W, 2S, 3S, 6E
6. W R I S T S
   2S, 5N, 5W, 4S, 2S, 3E

7. T H I G H S
   1E, 1S, 3W, 3N, 5E, 4S
8. E L B O W S
   5W, 2E, 2S, 2E, 3E, 1N
9. A N K L E S
   3E, 3S, 1E, 2N, 1W, 7W
10. S P I N E
    1S, 5E, 6+6W, 4W, 3S
11. H A N D S
    2E, 4W, 2+2S, 5N, 3E
12. C A L V E S
    2N, 1E, 5W, 1S, 1N+1E, 1N

Page 6

Page 7

Listening/Following Directions　　Name _____

Find Your Way

Mary has invited some friends to visit her. Follow her written directions and draw the path her friends should take.

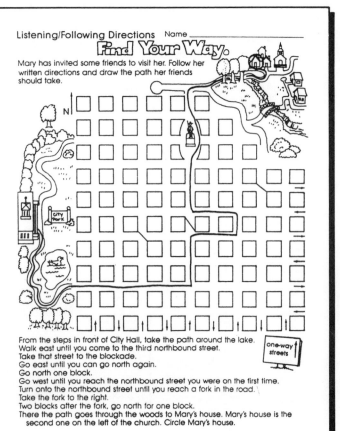

N

CITY PARK

one-way streets

From the steps in front of City Hall, take the path around the lake.
Walk east until you come to the third northbound street.
Take that street to the blockade.
Go east until you can go north again.
Go north one block.
Go west until you reach the northbound street you were on the first time.
Turn onto the northbound street until you reach a fork in the road.
Take the fork to the right.
Two blocks after the fork, go north for one block.
There the path goes through the woods to Mary's house. Mary's house is the second one on the left of the church. Circle Mary's house.

Page 7

Page 8

Listening/Following Directions　　Name _____

2-4-6-8 Who Do We Appreciate?

Use the following number sequence as directed.
2, 4, 6, 8, 10, 12, 14, 16, 18, 20, 22, 24, 26, 28, 30, 32
Cross out each number as you use it.

68

1.	32	6	4	26
2.	10	20	22	16
3.	18	12	14	24
4.	8	30	28	2

68

Write the lowest number of the number sequence in the bottom right space.
Write the largest number in the top left square.
Write the eighth lowest number in the right space of the second row.
Write the third largest number in the third space of the fourth row.
Write the only number divisible by eleven in the third space of the second row.
Write the second number in the sequence in the third space of the top row.
Write the fifth lowest number in the left space of the second row.
Write two times seven in the only space left in the third column.
Write the fourth largest number in the top right space.
Write the largest number that remains in the second space in the bottom row.
Write the fourth lowest number in the bottom left space.
Write the fifth highest number in the right space of the third row.
Write the third lowest number in the second space in the top row.
Write the lowest remaining number in the second space in the third row.
Write the lowest remaining number in the left space of the third row.
Write the only remaining number in the second space of the second row.
Add the numbers in row one. Write the answer in the box.
Add the numbers in the left column. Write the answer in the triangle.
Add the numbers on the diagonal from the top left space to the bottom right space. Write the answer in the circle.
Do all the other columns, rows and diagonals equal the same number? _____
Show proof of your answer.
Can you duplicate this using a different sequence? Try it.

Page 8

Answer Key

Listening/Following Directions   Name _____

Co-De-Tective

A equals 2. After that every other letter of the alphabet is an even number. (2, 4, 6, etc.)
B equals 1. Every other letter after B is an odd number. (3, 5, 7, etc.)
Write the number for each letter of the alphabet under it.

A B C D E F G H I J K L M N O P Q R S T U V W X Y Z
2 1 4 3 6 5 8 7 10 9 12 11 14 13 16 15 18 17 20 19 22 21 24 23 26 25

1. Write the number of inches in a yard. 36
2. Draw six squares. Mark the fourth one with an x.

☐ ☐ ☐ ☒ ☐ ☐

3. Write the date and year of your birth and where you were born.
   (answers will vary)

4. Draw an oval lengthwise in the middle of the box. Make a funny animal from it.

(artwork)

1. 24-17-10-19-6   19-7-6   13-22-14-1-6-17   16-5   10-13-4-7-6-20   10-13   2
   26-2-17-3.
2. 3-17-2-24   20-10-23   20-18-22-2-17-6-20   14-2-17-12   19-7-6   5-16-22-17-19-7
   16-13-6   24-10-19-7   2-13   23.
3. 24-17-10-19-6   19-7-6   3-2-19-6   2-13-3   26-6-2-17   16-5   26-16-22-17
   1-10-17-19-7   2-13-3   24-6-17-6   26-16-22   24-6-17-6   1-16-17-13.
4. 3-17-2-24   2-13   16-21-2-11   11-6-13-8-19-7-24-10-20-6   10-13   19-7-6
   14-10-3-3-11-6   16-5   19-7-6   1-16-23.   14-2-12-6   2   5-22-13-13-26
   2-13-10-14-2-11   5-17-16-14   10-19.

Listening/Following Directions   Name _____

Far Out

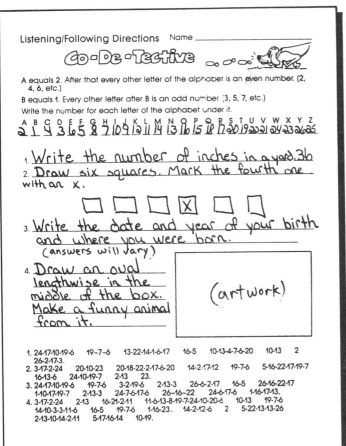

Draw a line through the name of the fourth planet from the sun.
Mark an X on your planet.
Draw a line under the planet with rings.
Draw a circle around the seventh planet from the sun.
Make an X above the middle planet.
Draw a triangle around the smallest planet.
Color in Earth's neighboring planets.
Make an X under the planet farthest from Earth.
Draw a line through the planet second farthest from the farthest planet.
Write a capital L on the largest planet.
Circle the name of the hottest planet.
Cross out the word on the diagram that is not a planet's name.
Underline the names of the planets whose names are spelled with the same
   letters except one.
Number the planets alphabetically on the line next to their names.
Earth's letters can be arranged to spell two other words. What are they?

heart hater

Write the names of the planets in order according to their size. Jupiter, Saturn, Uranus, Neptune, Mars, Pluto, Venus, Earth, Mercury

Listening/Following Directions   Name _____

Famous Scientists

Follow the directions to write the name of each scientist.

An Astronomer	A Chemist
G A L I L E O	P A S T E U R
1 2 3 4 5 6 7	8 9 10 11 12 13 14

A Doctor	A Physicist
B A R N A R D	E I N S T E I N
15 16 17 18 19 20 21	22 23 24 25 26 27 28 29

A Botanist	A Mathematician
C A R V E R	N E W T O N
30 31 32 33 34 35	36 37 38 39 40 41

On line 33, use the fourth letter in crevice.
On lines 10 and 25, use the letter that makes the /s/ sound.
On lines 3 and 5, use the consonant after K in the alphabet.
On lines 14, 17, 20, 32 and 35, use the third letter in agreeable.
On line 38, use the letter that looks like a capital M upside down.
On line 1, use the consonant before H in the alphabet.
On lines 6, 12, 22, 27, 34 and 37, use the first vowel in the third syllable of influence.
On line 15, use the consonant that appears twice in abominable.
On lines 18, 24, 29, 36 and 41, use the fourteenth letter of the alphabet.
On lines 2, 9, 16, 19 and 31, use the silent letter in the second syllable of approach.
On lines 7 and 40, use the letter between N and P.
On lines 4, 23 and 28, use the fifth letter from the end of quickly.
On line 8, use the silent consonant in pneumonia.
On lines 11, 26 and 39, use the middle letter in heather.
On line 21, use the double letter in riddle.
On line 30, use the first consonant in the second syllable of acorn.
On line 13, use the sixth letter from the end of the alphabet.

Listening/Following Directions   Name _____

Start to Finish

Follow the directions for each of the following sequences.

Answers will vary.

Write a number. _____
Double it. _____
Add 120 ÷ 30. _____
Multiply by 83 − 78. _____
Add a dozen. _____
Multiply by a tenth of one hundred. _____
Subtract 320. _____
Cross out the last two digits. What is the number? _____
Try this again with another number in the column at the right. _____

Write a number. _____
Double it. _____
Add 45 − 28. _____
Subtract one-third of nine. _____
Divide by 54 ÷ 9 − 4. _____
Subtract the original number. _____
Try this again with another number in the column at the right. _____

Write a number. _____
Multiply it by the number of sides in a triangle. _____
Add 6 × 4 ÷ 8 − 2. _____
Multiply by 63 ÷ 9 − 4. _____
Add the original number. _____
Subtract the number of legs on a tripod. _____
Cross out the last digit. What is the number? _____
Try this again with another number in the column at the right. _____

        IF8712 Reading Skills

Answer Key

Page 13

Listening/Following Directions   Name _____

World Capitals

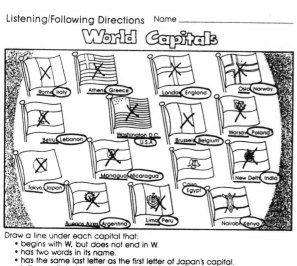

Draw a line under each capital that:
- begins with W, but does not end in W.
- has two words in its name.
- has the same last letter as the first letter of Japan's capital.
- is the capital of a country whose name begins with P and ends in U.
- begins with the same letter as the country to which it is the capital.
- contains three A's in its name.
- is the capital of an island country.
- is a homonym of a word that means to wander.
- has the same first and last letter.
- has the same name as a city in Georgia

The two capitals not underlined are **Cairo and Nairobi**

On what continent are they? **Africa** _____ Write the names of three other
countries on that continent. **South Africa, Algeria, Chad** (Answers will vary)

Circle the names of the countries. Write their capitals in alphabetical order.

**Athens, Beirut, Brussels, Buenos Aires, Cairo, Lima, London,
Managua, Nairobi, New Delhi, Oslo, Rome, Tokyo, Warsaw, Wash. D.C.**

Page 13

Page 14

Sequencing   Name _____

Timely Words

Read each sentence. Circle the two words which tell when something happens. Write each circled word on the correct line to show which word would come before or after the other word in time.

1. Mike hopes to (someday) visit Washington D.C., but (meanwhile) he reads books about the capital city.
   before **meanwhile**   after **someday**

2. Some of the tourists left (immediately) for the airport while others planned to leave (later) in the day.
   before **immediately**   after **later**

3. Although John has put off mowing the yard for (now) he knows he must (eventually) get it done.
   before **now**   after **eventually**

4. Kim said she would have arrived (sooner) but she waited for a phone call that (finally) came.
   before **sooner**   after **finally**

5. Tom wanted to appear (earlier) in the play, but his character did not appear until the (last) scene.
   before **earlier**   after **last**

6. The photographer said that Sally would have her picture taken (first) but that Kevin would be (next.)
   before **first**   after **next**

Circle the word that would come before the other word. Use the circled word in a sentence.

1. eventually (previously): **Answers will vary.**

2. (immediately) later: _____

3. (earlier) last: _____

Page 14

Page 15

Sequencing   Name _____

Timely Events

Read each sentence about two events. One event should happen before the other. Write each event on the correct line.

1. When you have completed your assignment, place your report in the basket on the teacher's desk.
   Before: **When you have completed your assignment,**
   After: **place your report on the teacher's desk.**

2. The golfers plan to finish the last four holes as soon as the rain stops.
   Before: **as soon as the rain stops.**
   After: **The golfers plan to finish the last four holes**

3. Before the rush hour traffic began, Ed rode his bike to the mall to buy a new pair of tennis shoes.
   Before: **Before the rush hour traffic began,**
   After: **Ed rode his bike to the mall to buy a new pair of tennis shoes.**

4. After returning from a visit to his aunt and uncle's ranch, Paul wrote them a long thank you letter.
   Before: **After returning from a visit to his aunt and uncle's ranch,**
   After: **Paul wrote them a long thank you letter.**

5. The day after his twenty-first birthday, Meg's cousin inherited fifty thousand dollars.
   Before: **The day after his twenty-first birthday,**
   After: **Meg's cousin inherited fifty thousand dollars.**

6. The scouts collected money for a month to buy clothes and toys for needy kids.
   Before: **The scouts collected money for a month**
   After: **to buy clothes and toys for needy kids.**

Page 15

Page 16

Sequencing   Name _____

Look What I've Made!

Read each invention on the time line. Write 1-15 to put the dates in order. Write each date by an invention starting from the earliest to the latest date.

1. safety pin **1849**
2. typewriter **1867**
9. helicopter **1907**
3. telephone **1876**
10. television **1920**
5. zipper **1893**
4. skyscraper **1884**
6. radio **1895**
13. polio vaccine **1952**
12. transistor **1947**
11. jet engine **1939**
8. airplane **1903**
7. x-ray **1895**
14. satellite **1957**
15. laser **1960**

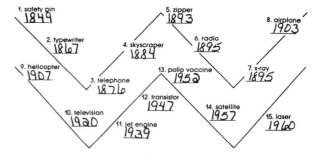

(9) 1907 (4) 1884 (10) 1920 (1) 1849 (15) 1960 (8) 1903 (3) 1876 (5) 1893
(14) 1957 (6) 1895 (13) 1952 (7) 1895 (2) 1867 (12) 1947 (11) 1939

Write before or after on each line.
The transistor was invented **before** the laser.
The polio vaccine was invented **after** the x-ray.
The helicopter was invented **after** the airplane.
The jet engine was invented **after** the safety pin.
The radio was invented **before** the television.
The zipper was invented **after** the typewriter.
The telephone was invented **before** the skyscraper.

Page 16

Answer Key

Page 17

Hail to the Chief!

Selecting a president of the United States can be a very elaborate process. It officially begins in the summer of the election year when the two major parties (Democrats and Republicans) hold their conventions. They each select a candidate for president and vice president. During the next few months, the candidates campaign across the country. Then on the first Tuesday following the first Monday of November, the election is held. Shortly thereafter, the Electoral College meets to confirm the winner. Early in January, after the election in November, members of Congress meet to officially count the Electoral College votes. On January 20th, Inauguration Day, the elected president takes the same oath of office that was taken by George Washington.

*Write 1-6 to put the major presidential election events in the correct order.

- (6) Inauguration
- (2) Campaign
- (4) Electoral College
- (3) Election
- (1) Nomination
- (5) Congress Confirms

On the lines below, write the specific steps (in order) in electing a president of the United States.

1. *Each party selects a candidate at their convention.*
2. *The candidates campaign.*
3. *The election is held on the 1st Tues. following the 1st Mon. of Nov.*
4. *The Electoral College meets to confirm the winner.*
5. *Congress meets in Jan. to count the Electoral College votes.*
6. *On Jan. 20th, the elected president takes the oath of office.*

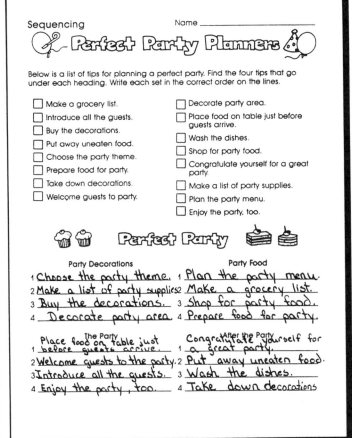

Page 18

Perfect Party Planners

Below is a list of tips for planning a perfect party. Find the four tips that go under each heading. Write each set in the correct order on the lines.

- ☐ Make a grocery list.
- ☐ Introduce all the guests.
- ☐ Buy the decorations.
- ☐ Put away uneaten food.
- ☐ Choose the party theme.
- ☐ Prepare food for party.
- ☐ Take down decorations.
- ☐ Welcome guests to party.
- ☐ Decorate party area.
- ☐ Place food on table just before guests arrive.
- ☐ Wash the dishes.
- ☐ Shop for party food.
- ☐ Congratulate yourself for a great party.
- ☐ Make a list of party supplies.
- ☐ Plan the party menu.
- ☐ Enjoy the party, too.

Perfect Party

Party Decorations
1. Choose the party theme.
2. Make a list of party supplies.
3. Buy the decorations.
4. Decorate party area.

Party Food
1. Plan the party menu.
2. Make a grocery list.
3. Shop for party food.
4. Prepare food for party.

The Party
1. Place food on table just before guests arrive.
2. Welcome guests to the party.
3. Introduce all the guests.
4. Enjoy the party, too.

After the Party
1. Congratulate yourself for a great party.
2. Put away uneaten food.
3. Wash the dishes.
4. Take down decorations

Page 19

Chef's Shuffle

Read the recipe carefully. Write 1-15 in the circles to put the cooking steps in the correct order.

Chocolate Soufflé

Break 3 ounces of German chocolate into pieces. Mix with 2 tablespoons of cold coffee. Place in the upper part of a double boiler and place over hot water on the stove. Stir until melted. Cool for 10 minutes.

Preheat oven to 325 degrees. Butter a 1½ quart soufflé dish. Separate 6 egg whites from the yolks. Beat egg whites until stiff. Add a dash of salt. Gradually add sugar and stir slowly. Add the cooled chocolate mixture and mix thoroughly. Pour into the soufflé dish. Place in oven and bake for 30-35 minutes. Serve immediately.

- (2) Mix chocolate with 2 tablespoons of cold coffee.
- (12) Add the cooled chocolate mixture and mix.
- (7) Butter a 1½ quart soufflé dish.
- (5) Cool mixture for ten minutes.
- (10) Add a dash of salt.
- (1) Break 3 ounces of German chocolate into pieces.
- (15) Serve immediately.
- (9) Beat the egg whites until stiff.
- (6) Preheat oven to 325 degrees.
- (13) Pour mixture into soufflé dish.
- (3) Place mixture in double boiler and place over hot water.
- (11) Add sugar to egg whites and stir slowly.
- (8) Separate 6 egg whites from the yolks.
- (4) Stir chocolate mixture until melted.
- (14) Place in oven and bake for 30-35 minutes.

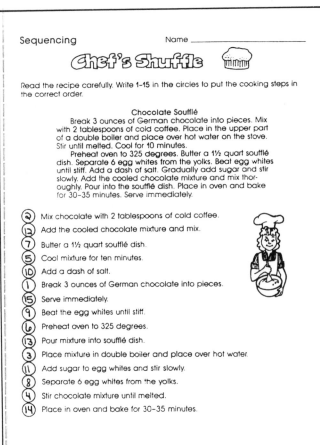

Page 20

What's Inside?

Read each book title. The titles give strong clues about the contents of the books. Choose each title that indicates that the book deals with sequencing. Write those titles on the lines.

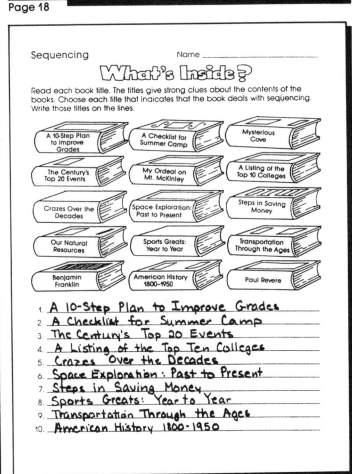

1. A 10-Step Plan to Improve Grades
2. A Checklist for Summer Camp
3. The Century's Top 20 Events
4. A Listing of the Top Ten Colleges
5. Crazes Over the Decades
6. Space Exploration: Past to Present
7. Steps in Saving Money
8. Sports Greats: Year to Year
9. Transportation Through the Ages
10. American History 1800-1950

Answer Key

Sequencing   Name _____

As the World Turns...

Read each major event in world history. Write each event in the correct order under the heading. (B.C. comes before the other dates. To put B.C. dates in order, count backwards. Ex: 2500 B.C. happened before 338 B.C.)

206 B.C.—The Great Wall of China built. 1920—Panama Canal opened. 1945 —United Nations founded. 27 B.C.—Augustus is first Roman emperor. 768— Charlemagne rules the Franks. 1914—World War I begins. 1815—Napolean defeated at Waterloo. 1865—U.S. Civil War ends. 1750 B.C.—Babylonian Empire begins. 1000—Ericson sails to America. 1869—Suez Canal opened. 1440—Invention of moveable type. 1969—Man walks on the moon. 331 B.C.— Alexander the Great defeats Persians. 1192—The first shogun rules Japan. 1920—League of Nations established. 1500 B.C.—Shang dynasty rules China. 1522—Magellan sails around world. 1492—Columbus discovers America. 1279 —Kublai Khan conquers China.

Famous World Events
Ancient Times (B.C. dates)
- 1750 BC: Babylonian Empire begins.
- 1500 BC: Shang dynasty rules china.
- 331 BC: Alexander the Great defeats Persians.
- 206 BC: The Great Wall of China built.
- 27 BC: Augustus is first Roman emperor.

Middle Ages (476-1450)
- 768: Charlemagne rules the Franks.
- 1100: Ericson sails to America.
- 1192: The first shogun rules Japan.
- 1279: Kublai Khan conquers China.
- 1440: Invention of moveable type.

Early Modern Times (1450-1900)
- 1492: Columbus discovered America.
- 1522: Magellan sails around the world.
- 1815: Napoleon defeated at Waterloo.
- 1865: U.S. Civil War ends.
- 1869: Suez Canal opened.

Modern Times (1900-
- 1914: World War I begins.
- 1920: League of Nations established.
- 1920: Panama Canal opened.
- 1945: United Nations founded.
- 1969: Man walks on the moon.

Page 21

Sequencing   Name _____

Look Where I've Been!

Read the list of explorations. Write 1–14 to put the events in sequence from the earliest to the most recent.

- 5 In 1513, Vasco de Balboa discovered the Pacific Ocean.
- 1 Eric the Red sailed from Iceland to Greenland in 982.
- 8 In 1535, Jacques Cartier sailed up the St. Lawrence River.
- 11 Robert Perry reached the North Pole in 1909.
- 3 In 1498, Vasco Da Gama reached India by sea.
- 7 Hernando Cortes conquered Mexico in 1519.
- 13 In 1963, Valentina Tereshkova became first the woman in space.
- 9 James Cook explored the South Pacific in 1768.
- 6 In 1519, Ferdinand Magellan sailed around the world.
- 10 William Clark crossed the Rocky Mountains in 1804.
- 4 In 1513, Ponce de Leon explored Florida.
- 2 Christopher Columbus sailed to America in 1492.
- 14 In 1969, Neil Armstrong became the first man on the moon.
- 12 Sir Edmund Hillary explored the South Pole in 1957.

Complete each statement with name(s) from above. Answers will vary.

Magellan and Cartier were explorers before James Cook.

Armstrong was an explorer after Sir Edmund Hillary.

Cortes and Magellan were explorers after Ponce de Leon.

Cook was an explorer before William Clark.

Eric the Red was an explorer before Columbus and Balboa was after him.

Page 22

Sequencing   Name _____

A Passport to Travel

At some time, you may decide to leave the country to travel in other countries. As an American citizen, you are free to leave the country at anytime. But to enter another country or re-enter the United States, you must have an official passport that identifies you as an American citizen. So, before you travel out of the country you will need to obtain a passport in the following way.

First, you must obtain an official copy of your birth certificate. Next, you must have your photo taken. It can be black and white or color, but it must be two inches by two inches in size. If you are not old enough for a driver's license, you will need a copy of your parent's license. Then you must obtain and fill out an official passport application form. Next, you should return the birth certificate, photo, driver's license and application to the passport office. You will then be asked to pay a fee for making your passport. The passport office will then process your information. Soon, you will obtain an official passport which will identify you as a citizen of the United States of America.

Rewrite the sentences on the lines to put the "steps to a passport" in order.
- Obtain and fill out an official passport application.
- Pay fee for passport.
- Obtain a copy of your birth certificate.
- You will have a United States passport.
- Passport office will process the information.
- Have a copy made of parent's driver's license.
- Return birth certificate, photo, license and application.
- Have a 2 x 2 inch photo taken.

1. Obtain a copy of your birth certificate.
2. Have a 2x2 inch photo taken.
3. Have a copy made of parent's driver's license.
4. Obtain and fill out an official passport application.
5. Return birth certificate, photo, license & application.
6. Pay fee for passport.
7. Passport office will process the information.
8. You will have a United States passport.

Page 23

Vocabulary   Name _____

Expansion

Write the words in the box after their appropriate category. Answers may vary.

frilly	unctuous	southeast	slither	pantry
reptiles	artist	depressed	adorned	luxurious
underhanded	inclined	rodents	gourmet	exhilarated
tricky	skimmed	affectionate	elaborate	insects
tramp	straight	deceitful	center	markers
acrylics	skyward	pastels	amble	culinary

Decorative Words frilly, adorned, elaborate, luxurious

Directional Words straight, southeast, center, skyward

Kitchen Words culinary, pantry, gourmet

Words That Can Bite rodents, insects, reptiles

Words for Feelings depressed, affectionate, deceitful, exhilarated

Words That Draw acrylics, artist, markers, pastels

Words That Move skimmed, amble, tramp, slither, inclined

Slippery Words tricky, underhanded, unctuous

A word is missing in each sentence below. Select a sensible word from above. Write it on the line in the sentence where it belongs.

1. The boat skimmed over the water to win the race.
2. The furnishings in the display house bedrooms were as frilly as a lamb's curly hair.
3. Mary usually uses acrylics because they look similar to, but are easier to use than oil paints.
4. Ted was inclined to take the path to the right although the directions said to go left.
5. The floor's surface had an elaborate covering after it was polished.
6. Our dog always gets depressed when he sees us packing suitcases.
7. Dad is a gourmet because he enjoys cooking and eating fine food.
8. The insects were especially annoying after the rain.

Page 24

Answer Key

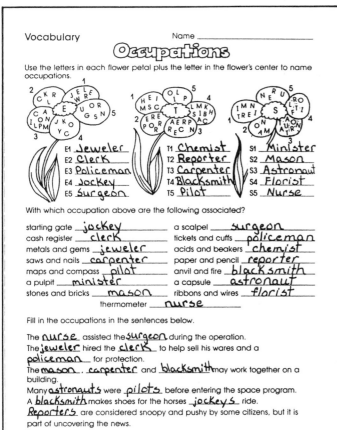

Vocabulary
Name _____

Occupations

Use the letters in each flower petal plus the letter in the flower's center to name occupations.

E1 Jeweler
E2 Clerk
E3 Policeman
E4 Jockey
E5 Surgeon

T1 Chemist
T2 Reporter
T3 Carpenter
T4 Blacksmith
T5 Pilot

S1 Minister
S2 Mason
S3 Astronaut
S4 Florist
S5 Nurse

With which occupation above are the following associated?

starting gate __jockey__
cash register __clerk__
metals and gems __jeweler__
saws and nails __carpenter__
maps and compass __pilot__
a pulpit __minister__
stones and bricks __mason__
thermometer __nurse__

a scalpel __surgeon__
tickets and cuffs __policeman__
acids and beakers __chemist__
paper and pencil __reporter__
anvil and fire __blacksmith__
a capsule __astronaut__
ribbons and wires __florist__

Fill in the occupations in the sentences below.

The __nurse__ assisted the __surgeon__ during the operation.
The __jeweler__ hired the __clerk__ to help sell his wares and a __policeman__ for protection.
The __mason__, __carpenter__ and __blacksmith__ may work together on a building.
Many __astronauts__ were __pilots__ before entering the space program.
A __blacksmith__ makes shoes for the horses __jockeys__ ride.
__Reporters__ are considered snoopy and pushy by some citizens, but it is part of uncovering the news.

Page 25

Vocabulary
Name _____

Paired Sense

Add one letter to each word below to form pairs of antonyms.

__h__ealthy
__w__arm
__l__ight
__s__cared
__b__egin
__s__and
__f__ront

__s__ickly
__c__old
__d__ark
__b__rave
__s__top
__o__cean
__b__ack

__s__mart
__m__iser
__r__aised
__m__assive
__h__onest
__f__alter
__f__riend

__s__tupid
__s__pender
__l__owered
__s__light
__c__rooked
__p__ersist
__e__nemy

Write the pair of antonyms that will fit in each sentence.

The veterinarian cared for the __sickly__ dog until he was __healthy__ again.
Some people would rather drive over __sand__ and sail over the __ocean__ than fly in a plane.
The workmen __raised__ their supplies over their heads before they __lowered__ them to the level on which they were working.
The amount of food was so __massive__ that no one noticed the __slight__ tear in the tablecloth.
The __brave__ boy climbed out on the limb of the tree to rescue the __scared__ cat.
Harry ran in the __front__ door and out the __back__ to get away from the angry bee.
On very __cold__ nights, we sit by the fire to keep __warm__.
When Kurt wants something, he __persists__ and does not __falter__.
My __friend__, Josh, plays basketball on the __enemy__ team.
You may __begin__ the test now and do not __stop__ until I tell you.
The __crooked__ employee was caught stealing by an __honest__ employee.
For a __smart__ person, he was __stupid__ to think that no one would steal from the open safe.
The __dark__ night had turned __light__ when the moon came out from behind the clouds.
I borrow from my sister, a __miser__, because I am a __spender__ and cannot save a thing.

Page 26

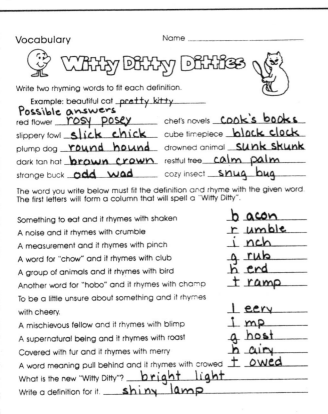

Vocabulary
Name _____

Witty Ditty Ditties

Write two rhyming words to fit each definition.

Example: beautiful cat __pretty kitty__

Possible answers
red flower __rosy posey__
slippery fowl __slick chick__
plump dog __round hound__
dark tan hat __brown crown__
strange buck __odd wad__

chef's novels __cook's books__
cube timepiece __block clock__
drowned animal __sunk skunk__
restful tree __calm palm__
cozy insect __snug bug__

The word you write below must fit the definition and rhyme with the given word. The first letters will form a column that will spell a "Witty Ditty".

Something to eat and it rhymes with shaken __b acon__
A noise and it rhymes with crumble __r umble__
A measurement and it rhymes with pinch __i nch__
A word for "chow" and it rhymes with club __g rub__
A group of animals and it rhymes with bird __h erd__
Another word for "hobo" and it rhymes with champ __t ramp__
To be a little unsure about something and it rhymes with cheery. __l eery__
A mischievous fellow and it rhymes with blimp __i mp__
A supernatural being and it rhymes with roast __g host__
Covered with fur and it rhymes with merry __h airy__
A word meaning pull behind and it rhymes with crowed __t owed__

What is the new "Witty Ditty"? __bright light__
Write a definition for it. __shiny lamp__

Page 27

Vocabulary
Name _____

Comparisons

A simile compares things which have something in common and still are often quite different. One thing is compared with another using as or like.

Jane is stubborn as a mule.

A metaphor states the comparison even stronger.

Jane is a mule.

Jane is not a mule, but she is stubborn. A characteristic of mules is their stubbornness. It is this characteristic that is being compared.

Complete the following similes. __Answers will vary.__

as sharp as a _____
as jumpy as a _____
as thin as a _____
as strong as a _____
as tenacious as a _____

climbs like a _____
shines like a _____
sounds like a _____
moves like a _____
talks like a _____

Do not use any of the verbs or adjectives from above as you continue.

as _____ as a ghost
as _____ as ice
as _____ as a bear
as _____ as a feather
as _____ as honey

_____ like a snake
_____ like a powder puff
_____ like falling leaves
_____ like a bird
_____ like a rusty gate

Write three sentences. Use a simile in each one to describe as directed.

The appearance of a roof _____
The size of a cut _____
The color of the sky _____

Draw a line under the metaphors in the sentences below.

The river was a fence around the pasture.
Sandra's nose was bent out of shape when she was not elected class president.
The loss of her dog broke Kristen's head.
Grandma's arthritic fingers were all thumbs when it came to opening small jars.
They sat on a time bomb waiting for the results of the medical tests.

Page 28

Answer Key

Page 29

Vocabulary — Name _____

It Figures...

Idioms say one thing, but mean something else. Use the meanings listed below. Write the number of each meaning on the line next to the sentence in which the idiom it defines is used.

1. Rumors circulate quickly
2. Elated
3. In a quandary
4. Acted in a determined way
5. Twenty-four hours continuously
6. Lost the opportunity
7. Wildly disruptive
8. Made a foolish remark
9. Forgave each other
10. Believe only half of what is said
11. A forecast that something bad will occur
12. Rough times
13. Got angry
14. Got married
15. Really sad
16. Talk together

__3__ John was in the dark about what to fix for dinner.

__7__ The class was bouncing off the wall when the substitute told them to take their seats.

__14__ Michael and Karen finally tied the knot last Friday.

__6__ Henry missed the boat when he turned down a job in the White House.

__8__ Gale really put her foot in her mouth when she met the new neighbor.

__4__ John took the bull by the horns when he saw two boys beating a stray cat.

__2__ The graduating class was flying high after their final exams.

__12__ Terry had some hard knocks growing up in the big city.

__16__ Mom always chews the fat with the neighbor after everyone has gone in the morning.

__5__ Fido waited around the clock for his master to return from a business trip.

__15__ The entire school was down in the dumps after they were defeated by their closest rival.

__13__ Sandy lost his cool when he missed the last bus.

__11__ Although the handwriting was on the wall, Emily went ahead with her plans.

__9__ Justin and Marty buried the hatchet once the debate was settled.

__1__ Tongues were wagging when the principal was seen talking to several students.

__10__ You have to take what you hear with a grain of salt.

Page 29

Page 30

Vocabulary — Name _____

Oops! Look Alikes!

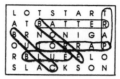

Find the word in the puzzle that will fit into two sentences below. Circle it and write it where it belongs. (The word only appears once in the puzzle, but it will be used twice below.)

1. Mother prepared the __batter__ for pancakes.
2. The wind messed up the __part__ in my hair.
3. Wally was really __blue__ when his dog was struck by a car.
4. Sean's pet __parrot__ can say "hello", "good-bye" and "I like you".
5. Molly tried out for the leading __part__ in the spring play.
6. The __batter__ struck out for the second time.
7. The boys' __club__ meets every other Tuesday in Seth's tree house.
8. A __blue__ bird built a nest in the hole of the old oak tree.
9. The gang had a __club__ they used to beat down the door.
10. The meeting was a total __bore__.
11. Tina's little brother likes to __parrot__ everything she says.
12. Charles __bore__ right through the wall with the screwdriver.

Write the sentence number in which the homograph being defined is located.

__4__ a bird
__1__ mixture of flour, eggs and milk
__6__ a baseball player
__3__ sad
__11__ imitate
__2__ separation
__10__ dull
__7__ organization
__9__ implement
__12__ drill
__8__ color
__5__ role

Write the homograph from the box to the right that can have either meaning.

drawing of earth; plan in detail __map__
chirp; peek through narrow opening __peep__
land along river's edge; place to keep money __bank__
small piece of paper; game __tag__
tall grass; mouthpiece for a woodwind instrument __reed__

REED	PEEP
MAP	BANK
TAG	

Page 30

Page 31

Vocabulary — Name _____

Oops! Sound Alikes!

Write the homophone or homonym for the following:

kernel __colonel__   naval __naval__
bald __bawled__   quarts __quartz__
need __knead__   fair __fare__
patients __patience__   jam __jamb__
vain __vein__   earn __urn__
idle __idol__   you __ewe__
liar __lyre__   read __red (or reed)__

Write two homophones or homonyms for the following:

scents __since, sense__   two __to, too__   rain __rein, reign__
there __their, they're__   way __weigh, whey__

Use a homophone or homonym pair from above in each sentence.

The __vain__ woman was upset when a __vein__ became raised on her hand.

What is the __fare__ for entrance to the __fair__?

The __colonel__ choked on a __kernel__ of corn.

The __liar__ said he could play the __lyre__ when he couldn't.

The __naval__ officer's __navel__ was injured when he fell from the deck onto the dock.

Nursing requires a great deal of __patience__ when caring for many __patients__.

George had to __earn__ a lot of money to buy the __urn__ his mother wanted for her birthday.

We __need__ to __knead__ the dough before we let it rise.

The __bald__ man __bawled__ when he saw his new car roll into the path of an oncoming truck.

Page 31

Page 32

Vocabulary — Name _____

Noun and Verb Clusters

The answers to the definitions go in the clusters clockwise around their number. Words will overlap. Some letters have been put in squares to get you started.

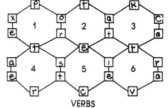

1. Send out of the country
2. Turn around
3. Go after with force
4. Provide with free sweets
5. Choose
6. Go from place to place

VERBS

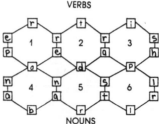

1. A piece of farm machinery
2. Person who buys and sells
3. Church community
4. A fruit
5. Piece of hair, string or yarn
6. Supernatural being

NOUNS

Use the words above to fill in the blanks in the sentences below.

South America __exports__ __bananas__ to other parts of the world.
The mysterious __spirit__ seemed to __attack__ at midnight.
People __travel__ far to attend the __parish__ in Green County.
It was difficult to __select__ the right __strand__ of yarn to finish the sweater.
The __reaper__'s back wheels __rotate__ in reverse in wet mud.
The __trader__ often __treats__ his customers to milk and cookies.

Page 32

Answer Key

Main Idea

Simply Amazing H's

Name _____

Read each paragraph. Put one line under the sentence which tells the main idea. Put two lines under the sentences which tell supportive ideas. Put a check by the best title for the paragraph.

Heart: <u>The heart is probably the most amazing and efficient machine in existence.</u> <u><u>It pumps blood through sixty thousand miles of arteries, veins and capillaries. During a lifetime, it will pump enough blood to fill the fuel tanks of over two thousand 747 jet planes.</u></u>

☐ The Heart Pumps Gallons of Blood
☑ The Heart: An Incredible Machine
☐ A Lifetime Pump

Height: <u>As we sleep, our bodies grow taller.</u> <u><u>The discs in our spine absorb fluid like a sponge, making the spine longer. While awake the liquid is squeezed out as we stand and move, causing the spine to shorten again.</u></u>

☐ Moveable Spines
☐ Sleepwalking
☑ Taller in Our Sleep

Handedness: <u>Most people in the world are right-handed.</u> <u><u>An average of 91 percent of the world's population uses their right hand mainly. From studying ancient art, scientists believe that this was true in ancient times, too.</u></u>

☑ A Right-Handed World
☐ Ancient Handwriting
☐ How Most People Write

Page 33

Main Idea

Making a List...

Name _____

Read each list below. Decide what the best heading for each list would be. Write the heading on the line. Possible answers.

Good Luck Superstitions
1. Finding a four-leaf clover
2. Carrying a rabbit's foot
3. Finding a penny heads up
4. Sleeping with a silver dollar under your mattress
5. Finding a horseshoe

Cities With "Love"
1. Loveland, Oklahoma
2. Lovelady, Texas
3. Lovejoy, Illinois
4. Love, Mississippi
5. Lovepoint, Maryland

Pro Baseball Teams
1. Los Angeles Dodgers
2. New York Mets
3. Chicago Cubs
4. St. Louis Cardinals
5. Cleveland Indians

Candy
1. Reese's Pieces
2. Snickers
3. Butterfinger
4. Almond Joy
5. 3 Musketeers

Statistics About Children
1. There are almost 2 billion children in the world.
2. In the U.S., one out of every 1,000 children works.
3. 1 billion children in the world do not finish elementary school.
4. Over 250 million children in the world are poor.
5. It can cost over $150,000 to raise a child to age 18.

"Star Trek" Characters
1. Captain Kirk
2. Doctor McCoy ("Bones")
3. Mr. Spock
4. Lt. Uhura
5. Chekhov

Complete the list of:
5 Ways Kids Can Make a Better World

1. **Answers will vary.**   2. _____
3. _____   4. _____
            5. _____

Page 34

Main Idea

I Didn't Know That!

Name _____

Read each paragraph. Put a check by the main idea. Underline two supportive ideas in the paragraph. On the line, write an appropriate title for each. Title answers will vary.

In 1974, an attempt was made to communicate with alien intelligence thousands of light years away. <u>From an observatory in Puerto Rico, a powerful radar beam was used to broadcast a three-minute message into outer space.</u> <u>It will take 50,000 light years to receive a reply, if there is one.</u>

☐ Radar's best use is for alien communication.
☑ Radar beams have given us a chance to explore other life in the universe.

Perhaps the most incredible tunnel system ever built was constructed in Vietnam during their war with France. <u>Called the Cu Chi network, it stretched for 150 miles.</u> <u>The tunnel system, which took thirty years to build by hand, contained a hospital, livestock and thousands of soldiers.</u>

☑ An elaborate tunnel system was built by hand in Vietnam.
☐ The Cu Chi network of tunnels is now used for traveling.

Time capsules are an intriguing way of leaving a record of our time for the future. <u>One time capsule was buried in 1964 at the World's Fair in New York.</u> <u>It contains among other things: a Bible, freeze-dried food, a Beatles' record and an electric toothbrush. It is to be opened in 5000 years!</u>

☐ Time capsules should contain important objects.
☑ Time capsules can leave clues of our culture to the future.

Page 35

Main Idea

Facinating Facts

Name _____

Read each paragraph. The main idea is somewhere in the paragraph. It may be at the beginning, middle or end of the paragraph. Find and underline the main idea in each paragraph. Put a check by the best title for each paragraph.

By studying rapid eye movements during sleep, scientists have discovered dreaming patterns of humans and animals. Cold-blooded animals such as fish and reptiles do not dream. <u>Warm-blooded animals such as mammals and birds do dream.</u>

☑ Dreams of Mammals
☐ Patterns of Dreaming
☐ Rapid Eye Movements

On a sunny day, the gleam from the World Trade Center in New York City can be seen two states away. The center contains enough concrete to form a path from New York to Washington, D.C. It has enough electrical wire to reach Mexico. It even has its own zip code. <u>The New York City World Trade Center is one of the tallest buildings in the world.</u>

☐ An Incredible View
☐ From New York to Mexico
☑ An Amazing Building

The first recorded Siamese twins were born in 945 A.D. <u>Throughout history other Siamese twin births have been recorded.</u> Siamese twins occur in as few as one in 200,000 births. Born in the Kingdom of Siam in 1811, Chang and Eng are two of the most famous twins.

wow!

☑ Siamese Twins
☐ Chang and Eng
☐ Twin Births

Page 36

Answer Key

Page 37

Main Idea   Name _____

The Fact of the Matter

Read each paragraph. Put one line under the main idea. Put two lines under the sentences which tell supportive ideas. In your own words, write the main idea on the line.

Shorthand

Shorthand, a system of quick writing, has been used since the year 63 B.C. A Roman named Marcus Tiro invented a system which remained in use for over 600 years. One of the symbols & is still used today.

main idea: _____ Answers will vary.

money

The world's oldest money was issued in China in 2697 B.C. The bank notes were called "flying money" or convenient money. It was printed on paper made from the mulberry tree. Blue ink was used.

main idea: _____

hibernation

Animal hibernation is one of nature's most amazing mysteries. Bears can sleep for five months without eating or drinking. Other animals, such as woodchucks, squirrels and some reptiles sleep so soundly that they can be picked up and tossed without waking them.

main idea: _____

elephants

A white elephant is considered a symbol of good luck in Thailand. It is a law that any white elephant found in Thailand must be given to the king. White elephants are really gray elephants which have pink eyes.

main idea: _____

Page 37

Page 38

Drawing Conclusions   Name _____

I Would Conclude...

Read each fact below. Put a check by the correct conclusion on each line. Write another conclusion for each fact.

1. Only one person is known to have ever been hit by a meteorite.
   - ☐ Meteorites usually fall in forests, lakes or hills.
   - ☑ The chances of being hit by a meteorite are almost zero.

   _____ Answers will vary.

2. A "jiffy" is defined as one hundred thousand billion billionths of a second.
   - ☑ A jiffy is an incredibly short period of time.
   - ☐ A jiffy is enough time for a quick phone call.

3. President George Washington died on the last hour of the last day of the last week of the last month of the last year of the eighteenth century (1700's).
   - ☐ President Washington died December 7, 1799.
   - ☑ President Washington died December 31, 1799.

4. An average golf course requires at least 400,000 gallons of water a week to stay green.
   - ☐ A golf course is heavily watered twice a week.
   - ☑ It takes a tremendous amount of water to keep a golf course green.

5. Killer bees have been responsible for killing almost three hundred persons in Brazil since 1957.
   - ☑ Killer bees are especially threatening to people in Brazil.
   - ☐ Killer bees pose a worldwide threat to people.

Page 38

Page 39

Drawing Conclusions   Name _____

Yesterday to the Future

Use the three calendars to help fill in each blank below.

year **1800**

S	M	T	W	T	F	S
						1
2	3	4	5	6	7	8
9	10	11	12	13	14	15
16	17	18	19	20	21	22
23	24	25	26	27	28	

1900

S	M	T	W	T	F	S
				1	2	3
4	5	6	7	8	9	10
11	12	13	14	15	16	17
18	19	20	21	22	23	24
25	26	27	28			

year **2000**

S	M	T	W	T	F	S
		1	2	3	4	5
6	7	8	9	10	11	12
13	14	15	16	17	18	19
20	21	22	23	24	25	26
27	28	29				

1. Each of the calendars shows the second month of the year. That month is **February**.
2. The first and third months are 100 years before and after 1900. Write the year above each month.
3. In this year, Valentine's Day (Feb. 14) would come on a Wednesday. The year must be **1900**.
4. In this year, the month would begin and end on the third day of the week. The year is **2000**.
5. In this year, the month would begin on the last day of the week and end on the sixth day of the week. The year is **1800**.
6. In the year 2000, George Washington's birthday would come exactly two weeks from February 8th. What day of the month and day of the week is it? **Tuesday, 22nd**
7. In the year 1900, Abraham Lincoln's birthday would be two days before Valentine's Day. What day would his birthday be? **Monday, 12th**
8. In the year 1800, what day of the week would the last day of January come on? **Friday**
9. In the year 2000, what day of the week would the first day of March come on? **Tuesday**
10. The 8th, 15th and 22nd days of the month are on Thursday. The year is **1900**.
11. If you had a birthday on the fourth Wednesday of February in the year 2000, what would your birthday be? **23rd**
12. Every four years is Leap Year which adds a day to February. The year **2000** would be a Leap Year.

Page 39

Page 40

Cause and Effect   Name _____

Cause and Effect

Read each sentence. Put a line under something that happened. (effect) Put two lines under the cause. Write 1 and 2 by cause and effect to tell their order in the sentence.

1. The museum opening was delayed for two weeks because they were waiting for the ancient artifacts to arrive.
       2 cause   **1** effect

2. Everyone was relieved when the artifacts arrived safely because they could so easily have been damaged in their crates.
       2 cause   **1** effect

3. Because the artifacts were breakable, they were placed behind glass cases so no one could touch them.
       1 cause   **2** effect

4. Because the artifacts were valued as priceless, the museum hired extra security guards to protect them.
       1 cause   **2** effect

5. Many people traveled from other cities and states to see the ancient exhibit because it had never been shown in this country.
       2 cause   **1** effect

6. Due to public demand, the museum decided to stay open each night from eight o'clock until eleven o'clock.
       1 cause   **2** effect

7. Special brochures and photos were available to the public because everyone wanted to learn as much as possible about the exhibit.
       2 cause   **1** effect

8. Because the artifacts exhibit was such a success, other museums asked for permission to show the exhibit, too.
       1 cause   **2** effect

Page 40

Answer Key

Page 41

Cause and Effect   Name _____

That's Why!

Read each sentence. Write two different things which <u>may</u> have caused the event in each sentence to happen. **Answers will vary.**

1. Effect: The train had left the station just before Jeff arrived.
   Cause I: *Jeff's car broke down.* _____
   Cause II: _____

2. Effect: The star basketball player could not play in the second half.
   Cause I: _____
   Cause II: _____

3. Effect: The line of cars came to a sudden stop on the narrow road.
   Cause I: _____
   Cause II: _____

4. Effect: The teacher returned Bob's paper and asked him to redo it.
   Cause I: _____
   Cause II: _____

5. Effect: The tourist stopped in the city to buy a new map.
   Cause I: _____
   Cause II: _____

6. Effect: Kate's mother stopped for gas on the way to the game.
   Cause I: _____
   Cause II: _____

7. Effect: Tom called Kevin to ask what their homework assignment was.
   Cause I: _____
   Cause II: _____

8. Effect: Meg was late for cheerleader practice Saturday morning.
   Cause I: _____
   Cause II: _____

Page 42

Inference   Name _____

Portrait Possibilities

Look at the portrait of the lady. Write 15 possibilities about the lady and her life that you feel must be true.

1. Answers will vary.
2. _____ 8. _____
3. _____ 9. _____
4. _____ 10. _____
5. _____ 11. _____
6. _____ 12. _____
7. _____ 13. _____
           14. _____
           15. _____

Page 43

Inference   Name _____

Autograph Please?

Read each book title in column B. Read the list of professions in column A. Write a letter on each line to tell which person probably wrote each book.

	A		B
b	1. a heart doctor	a.	Today's Education: A New Approach
m	2. a biologist	b.	Our Body's Amazing Pump
j	3. a concert pianist	c.	Behind My Presidential Campaign
e	4. a lawyer	d.	10 Ways to Make Them Say "I'll Buy It"
d	5. a salesperson	e.	Trial Tips
a	6. a school principal	f.	Let's Have Healthier Pets
n	7. an historian	g.	Secrets of the Universe
h	8. a tennis player	h.	Game, Set, Match!
o	9. a movie actor	i.	Laugh 'Til I Cry!
i	10. a comedian	j.	Chopin: His Life and His Music
f	11. a veterinarian	k.	Money Wise
c	12. a politician	l.	A Nose for News
l	13. a news reporter	m.	Plant and Animal Life of the Arctic
g	14. an astronomer	n.	Heroes of the American Revolution
k	15. a banker	o.	Hollywood Hints

Read each professional name below. Write the title of a book which could be written by each.

I. a sportscaster   Answers will vary.
II. a computer designer _____
III. an electrician _____
IV. a gardener _____
V. a mystery writer _____

Page 44

Inference   Name _____

See the U.S.A.

Read the table of contents from See the USA. Read each sentence taken from the book. Write the chapter and page number on each line to tell from where the quote is probably taken.

Ch. **II** page **48** Rolling clothes in plastic bags will prevent wrinkles.
Ch. **III** page **71** Some state parks will rent tents at a reasonable rate.
Ch. **I** page **36** Many wilderness parks exist in the northwest U.S.
Ch. **II** page **45** Traveler's checks are recommended for safety.
Ch. **III** page **62** Neat, clean rooms at a very reasonable rate.
Ch. **IV** page **75** Many airlines offer discounts for families.
Ch. **II** page **53** Allow two rolls of film for each sightseeing day.
Ch. **I** page **1** The southeast U.S. is especially lovely in the springtime.
Ch. **III** page **66** Some suites offer whirlpools in the bathrooms.
Ch. **IV** page **97** Special maps with trails marked can be ordered.
Ch. **II** page **55** Proper diet and enough rest will help you enjoy your trip.
Ch. **IV** page **78** Backseat games for children will help prevent boredom.
Ch. **IV** page **94** Some roads offer safety lanes for bikers.

Answer Key

Page 45

Inference   Name _____

Details Tell!

Look at each person. Write a sentence that tells what each detail tells about the person's personality, life, habits, interests, etc.

1. A. __Answers will vary.__
   B. _____
2. A. _____
   B. _____
3. A. _____
   B. _____
4. A. _____
   B. _____
5. A. _____
   B. _____
6. A. _____
   B. _____

Page 45

Page 46

Fact and Fantasy   Name _____

Switch!

Read each sentence. Underline fact or fantasy to describe each sentence. If the sentence is a fact, rewrite the sentence as fantasy. If the sentence is fantasy, rewrite the sentence as a fact. At the beginning of each new sentence, write fact or fantasy.   Sentences will vary.

1. fact or fantasy: Every four years an election is held to elect a President of the United States.
   __fact__ : _____

2. fact or fantasy: The Grand Canyon only appears to exist since it is really a mirage formed by waves of heat from the earth.
   __fantasy__ : _____

3. fact or fantasy: The United States is bordered on the east and west by the Atlantic and Pacific Oceans and by Canada and Mexico on the north and south.
   __fact__ : _____

4. fact or fantasy: The bottom of the ocean floor provides the ceiling for a hidden continent that lies under it.
   __fantasy__ : _____

5. fact or fantasy: As the cutter chopped each Christmas tree down, a larger more beautiful tree appeared in its place.
   __fantasy__ : _____

6. fact or fantasy: The famous Alamo still stands in San Antonio, Texas.
   __fact__ : _____

Page 46

Page 47

Fact and Fantasy   Name _____

Fact or Fantasy

Read each sentence. If it is a fact, circle the letter in column A. If it is a fantasy, circle the letter in column B. Write each circled letter on a line below.

		A	B
1.	At midnight, the island submerges in the water and then rises again.	g	(w)
2.	Newspapers, TV and radio are some ways of learning the daily news.	(r)	k
3.	Hydrogen and oxygen are names of gases.	(i)	b
4.	Four feet of new fallen snow covered the desert.	q	(t)
5.	The basketball player used special powers to make the ball go in the basket.	m	(e)
6.	Many families go on a vacation during the summer months.	(v)	x
7.	Dogs are believed to be spirits of ancient people.	c	(f)
8.	The hula hoop and pogo stick were popular fads.	(a)	r
9.	When blown, the whistle had the power to make everything stop.	h	(e)
10.	Computers can only do what they are programmed to do.	(n)	j
11.	When the man turned sideways, he could disappear.	p	(s)

__Write five facts__
1 2 3 4 5   7 3 6 5   7 8 9 4 11

1. _____
2. _____
3. _____
4. _____
5. _____

__Write five fantasies.__
1 2 3 4 5   7 3 6 5   7 8 10 4 8 11 3 5 11

1. _____
2. _____
3. _____
4. _____
5. _____

Page 47

Page 48

Fact and Opinion   Name _____

Facing the Facts

Some facts stay the same, while others may change. Read each fact below. On each line, write can change or cannot change.

1. __can change__   Sam's baby brother has two teeth.
2. __cannot change__   The United States is north of the equator.
3. __can change__   Jere's father and mother are 38 years old.
4. __cannot change__   The whale is the world's largest mammal.
5. __can change__   Kathleen has 697 stamps in her collection.
6. __can change__   The football uniforms are covered with mud.
7. __can change__   Molly has three overdue books from the library.
8. __cannot change__   Carrie is the oldest child in her family.
9. __cannot change__   Lettuce, potatoes and beans are vegetables.
10. __cannot change__   Steve's birthday is October 21st.
11. __cannot change__   The Earth has one moon in its orbit.
12. __can change__   The Harris family lives in Denver, Colorado.

__Possible answers.__
In the circles below, write each number of a fact from above that can change. Write a sentence about how it can change.

(1) __He can get more teeth.__
(3) __They can get older.__
(5) __She can get more.__
(6) __They can be washed.__
(7) __She can return them.__
(12) __They can move.__

Page 48

Answer Key

Fact and Opinion   Name _____

City Sights

Look at the scene below. Write ten facts and ten opinions about this city scene.

Answers will vary.

Facts

1. _____ 2. _____
3. _____ 4. _____
5. _____ 6. _____
7. _____ 8. _____
9. _____ 10. _____

Opinions

1. _____ 2. _____
3. _____ 4. _____
5. _____ 6. _____
7. _____ 8. _____
9. _____ 10. _____

Page 49

Fact and Opinion   Name _____

Judge These.

The lawyer is asking the witnesses many questions. Some of the answers are facts, some are opinions. The judge will only accept facts. Read each question and answer. Write fact or opinion on the lines by the names to describe their answers. **The students' written facts will vary.**

1. question: Mr. Wallace, what was the stranger wearing?
   answer: He was wearing a blue coat, red scarf, black slacks and black shoes.

2. question: Miss Raines, did you recognize the intruder?
   answer: How could I? He wore glasses so he wouldn't be recognized.

3. question: Mr. Henry, what did you hear from your window?
   answer: I heard a sound that must have been the intruder breaking in.

4. question: Ms. Harris, what time did you notice the broken lock?
   answer: It was 10:15 p.m., just as I arrived home.

5. question: Mrs. Patterson, do you know the owner of the stolen painting?
   answer: He is the nicest boss I have ever worked for.

6. question: Mr. Samuels, was the painting insured?
   answer: Yes, the painting was insured for ten thousand dollars.

7. question: Miss Ryan, did you see the defendant take the painting?
   answer: Of course he took it! It had to be him.

Mr. Wallace _fact_   Miss Raines _opinion_   Mr. Henry _opinion_
Ms. Harris _fact_   Mrs. Patterson _opinion_   Mr. Samuels _fact_
Miss Ryan _opinion_

*On the line under each answer, write another answer to the question. If the answer is a fact, write an opinion. If it is an opinion, write a fact.

Page 50

Fact and Opinion   Name _____

"State"-ments

Read each sentence about a state(s). On each line, write fact or opinion to describe each sentence.

fact 1. Alaska and Texas (a)re the two largest states in the U.S.
opinion 2. Flori(d)a is the best state for a summer vacation.
fact 3. Georgia is the largest state east of the Mississippi Ri(v)er.
fact 4. Hawaii is the only state completely surr(o)unded by water.
opinion 5. Col(o)rado has the nation's best ski slopes.
fact 6. Sacramento is the state capital of Califor(n)ia.
opinion 7. The desert(s) of Arizona are beautiful to paint.
fact 8. Minnesota's northern border (i)s next to Canada.
opinion 9. Wyoming has the friend(l)iest people in the U.S.
fact 10. New York Cit(y) is not the capital of New York state.
fact 11. Kansas and Nebraska are located in the mid(w)est.
opinion 12. Texas has the best state parks.
fact 13. R(h)ode Island is the smallest state.
opinion 14. It is (e)asy to find a job in Kentucky.
fact 15. New Jersey is called the Garden S(t)ate.

Use the circled letters from above to write the question.

W h a t   s t a t e   d o   y o u   l i v e   i n ?
11 13 1 15   7 15 1 15 14   2 5   10 5 4   9 3 14   8 6

_____

Write three facts and three opinions about your state.

Facts
1. _____
2. _____
3. _____

Opinions
1. _____
2. _____
3. _____

Page 51

Following Directions   Name _____

Art-i-Facts

Follow the directions to write the name of each artist responsible for each work of art.

R A P H A E L	R E M B R A N D T
14 7 5 12 7 10 1	14 10 9 4 14 7 11 16 6
"The Entombment"	"The Night Watch"
V A N G O G H	M I C H E L A N G E L O
2 7 11 8 13 8 12	9 15 3 12 10 1 7 11 8 10 1 13
"Sunflowers"	"Pieta"
D A V I N C I	E L G R E C O
16 7 2 15 11 3 15	10 1 8 14 10 3 13
"The Last Supper"	"The Burial of Count Orgaz"

1. Use the first consonant after the second vowel in ITALY.
2. Use the fifth consonant from the end of the alphabet.
3. Use the consonant that comes just after the two vowels together in MASTERPIECE.
4. Use the ninth letter before the eighth consonant in the alphabet.
5. Use the letter that comes just after the fourth vowel in the alphabet.
6. Use the consonant in ART that appears last in the alphabet.
7. Use the vowel that appears twice in CANVAS.
8. Use the fifth letter after the second vowel in PAINTING.
9. Use the consonant that comes between two vowels in FAMOUS.
10. Use the vowel that appears twice in the second syllable of FLORENCE.
11. Use the consonant that comes between the second vowel and third consonant in PAINTER.
12. Use the sixteenth consonant from the end of the alphabet.
13. Use the vowel in SCULPTOR which appears first in the alphabet.
14. Use the consonant which appears before and after the fourth letter in PORTRAIT.
15. Use the third vowel in RENAISSANCE.
16. Use the letter between the second consonant and second vowel of the alphabet.

Page 52

Answer Key

Page 53

Following Directions   Name _____

They're Noteworthy!

Some answers will vary.

Follow the directions for each sentence.

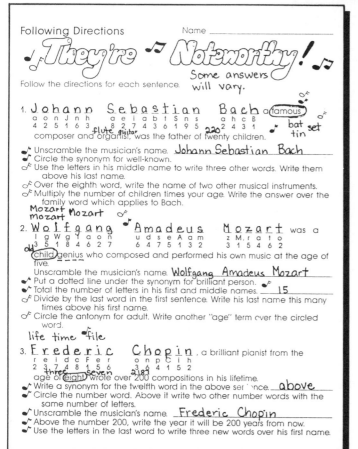

1. Johann Sebastian Bach a famous composer and organist, was the father of twenty children.
   - Unscramble the musician's name. Johann Sebastian Bach
   - Circle the synonym for well-known.
   - Use the letters in his middle name to write three other words. Write them above his last name.
   - Over the eighth word, write the name of two other musical instruments.
   - Multiply the number of children times your age. Write the answer over the family word which applies to Bach.

2. Wolfgang Amadeus Mozart was a child genius who composed and performed his own music at the age of five.
   - Unscramble the musician's name. Wolfgang Amadeus Mozart
   - Put a dotted line under the synonym for brilliant person.
   - Total the number of letters in his first and middle names. 15
   - Divide by the last word in the first sentence. Write his last name this many times above his first name.
   - Circle the antonym for adult. Write another "age" term over the circled word.

3. Frederic Chopin, a brilliant pianist from the age of eight wrote over 200 compositions in his lifetime.
   - Write a synonym for the twelfth word in the above sentence. above
   - Circle the number word. Above it write two other number words with the same number of letters.
   - Unscramble the musician's name. Frederic Chopin
   - Above the number 200, write the year it will be 200 years from now.
   - Use the letters in the last word to write three new words over his first name.

Page 54

Following Directions   Name _____

Tic-Tac-TRIVIA

Read each "Tic" question. Write each answer in the correct puzzle space. Then select the correct category for each question. Draw the symbol in the box in each puzzle space. Find the symbols which form a "Tic-Tac-Trivia" line. Draw a line.

| **l** : SPORTS | **X** : TV | **Ɛ** : CURRENT EVENTS | **◯** : SCIENCE |
| **+** : HISTORY | **✓** : GEOGRAPHY | | |

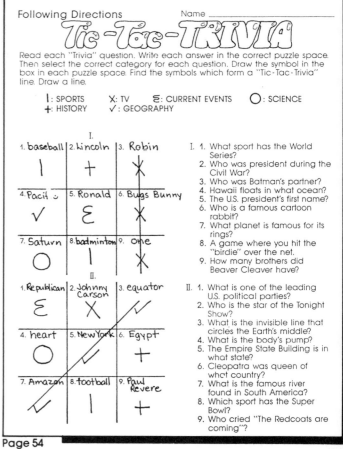

I. 1. What sport has the World Series?
2. Who was president during the Civil War?
3. Who was Batman's partner?
4. Hawaii floats in what ocean?
5. The U.S. president's first name?
6. Who is a famous cartoon rabbit?
7. What planet is famous for its rings?
8. A game where you hit the "birdie" over the net.
9. How many brothers did Beaver Cleaver have?

II. 1. What is one of the leading U.S. political parties?
2. Who is the star of the Tonight Show?
3. What is the invisible line that circles the Earth's middle?
4. What is the body's pump?
5. The Empire State Building is in what state?
6. Cleopatra was queen of what country?
7. What is the famous river found in South America?
8. Which sport has the Super Bowl?
9. Who cried "The Redcoats are coming"?

Page 55

Following Directions   Name _____

They're Ancient History Now!

Some answers will vary.

Follow the directions for each sentence.

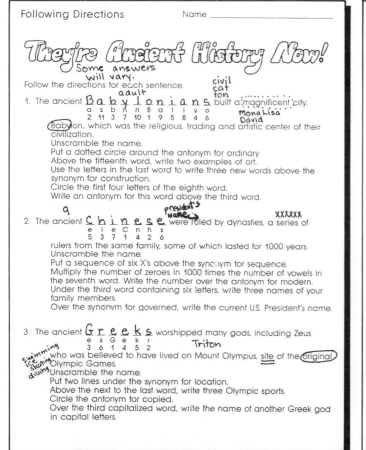

1. The ancient Babylonians built a magnificent city, Babylon, which was the religious, trading and artistic center of their civilization.
   - Unscramble the name.
   - Put a dotted circle around the antonym for ordinary.
   - Above the fifteenth word, write two examples of art.
   - Use the letters in the last word to write three new words above the synonym for construction.
   - Circle the first four letters of the eighth word.
   - Write an antonym for this word above the third word.

2. The ancient Chinese were ruled by dynasties, a series of rulers from the same family, some of which lasted for 1000 years.
   - Unscramble the name.
   - Put a sequence of six X's above the synonym for sequence.
   - Multiply the number of zeroes in 1000 times the number of vowels in the seventh word. Write the number over the antonym for modern.
   - Under the third word containing six letters, write three names of your family members.
   - Over the synonym for governed, write the current U.S. President's name.

3. The ancient Greeks worshipped many gods, including Zeus who was believed to have lived on Mount Olympus, site of the original Olympic Games.
   - Unscramble the name.
   - Put two lines under the synonym for location.
   - Above the next to the last word, write three Olympic sports.
   - Circle the antonym for copied.
   - Over the third capitalized word, write the name of another Greek god in capital letters.

Page 56

Following Directions   Name _____

Miles to Go...

Follow the directions to show the routes traveled.

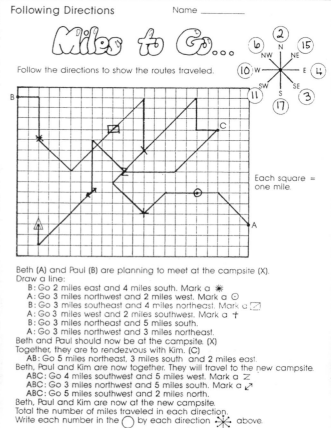

Each square = one mile.

Beth (A) and Paul (B) are planning to meet at the campsite (X). Draw a line:
- B: Go 2 miles east and 4 miles south. Mark a ✳
- A: Go 3 miles northwest and 2 miles west. Mark a ⊙
- B: Go 3 miles southeast and 4 miles northeast. Mark a ⊡
- A: Go 3 miles west and 2 miles southwest. Mark a +
- B: Go 3 miles northeast and 5 miles south.
- A: Go 3 miles northwest and 3 miles northeast.

Beth and Paul should now be at the campsite. (X)
Together, they are to rendezvous with Kim. (C)
- AB: Go 5 miles northeast, 3 miles south and 2 miles east.

Beth, Paul and Kim are now together. They will travel to the new campsite.
- ABC: Go 4 miles southwest and 5 miles west.
- ABC: Go 3 miles northwest and 5 miles south. Mark a Ƶ
- ABC: Go 5 miles southwest and 2 miles north.

Beth, Paul and Kim are now at the new campsite.
Total the number of miles traveled in each direction.
Write each number in the ◯ by each direction ✳ above.

Answer Key

Page 57

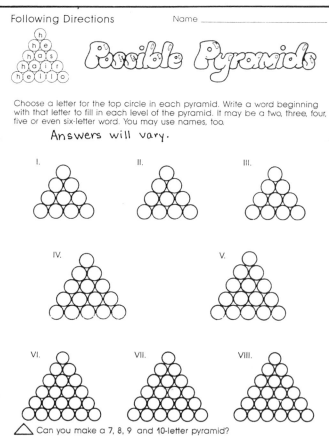

Following Directions   Name _____

Possible Pyramids

Choose a letter for the top circle in each pyramid. Write a word beginning with that letter to fill in each level of the pyramid. It may be a two, three, four, five or even six-letter word. You may use names, too.

Answers will vary.

I. II. III.

IV. V.

VI. VII. VIII.

△ Can you make a 7, 8, 9 and 10-letter pyramid?

Page 57

Page 58

Following Directions   Name _____

Wordly Endeavors

115	U	T	W	Q	M7	A	V	I	X	35	H	O	C
115	X	E	E	B	F4	Q	P	P	A	35	U	Z	O
V5	A	K	R	Y	R	Z	W	M	O	35	D	A	Y
15	H2O	E	R	B	A	L	X	X	X	N	N	OB	H
K5	H5O	L	O	K	F9	R	M	B	T	E	F	H	T
V5	H3O	B	R	I	T7	L	P	G	Y	D	I	I	J
N5	H2O	A2	A4	A8	A4	A6	40	40	A4	Y	F	R	S
F	H2O	N6	6	6	16	6	Q	N6	M	R	T	T	S
J	H5O	D	V	214	H	U	R	24	24	24	24	03	N

Find and mark each word in the following way:
1. **Find:** The thirty-fifth president of the U.S. elected in 1960.
   Write: 35 on any three letters in the name as long as one is a vowel.
2. **Find:** A word that rhymes with summarize which means "to voice a thought".
   Write: An X on the last three letters.
3. **Find:** A famous European city built on water canals.
   Write: The chemical sign for water - H_2O - on each letter.
4. **Find:** A word for a desert "sight" which really does not exist.
   Write: A cactus symbol 🌵 on the 1st, 2nd, 5th and 6th letters.
5. **Find:** One of the presidents carved on Mt. Rushmore in 1941.
   Write: The total of the numbers in 1941 on each letter.
6. **Find:** A synonym for mistake.
   Write: The correct letter in the square which contains the incorrect letter.
7. **Find:** A math term for a "part of a whole."
   Write: A different example of this term on each letter.
8. **Find:** The day of the week that the 24th would come on if the first day of the month came on Tuesday.
   Write: 24 on every letter that also appears in Tuesday.
9. **Find:** How many sides you would have if you totaled the sides in 6 triangles and 3 squares.
   Write: The total number backwards on the first and last letters.
10. **Find:** The number you would get by adding a zero to one hundred thousand.
    Write: The total number of zeroes on each letter.

Page 58

Page 59

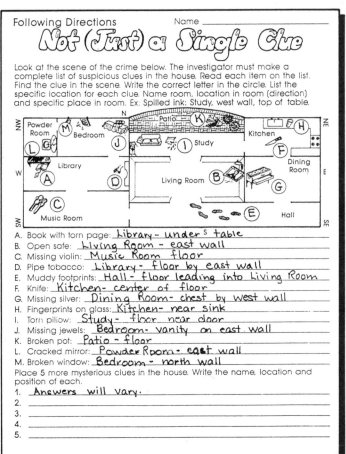

Following Directions   Name _____

Not (Just) a Single Clue

Look at the scene of the crime below. The investigator must make a complete list of suspicious clues in the house. Read each item on the list. Find the clue in the scene. Write the correct letter in the circle. List the specific location for each clue. Name room, location in room (direction) and specific place in room. Ex: Spilled ink: Study, west wall, top of table.

A. Book with torn page: **Library - under table**
B. Open safe: **Living Room - east wall**
C. Missing violin: **Music Room floor**
D. Pipe tobacco: **Library - floor by east wall**
E. Muddy footprints: **Hall - floor leading into Living Room**
F. Knife: **Kitchen - center of floor**
G. Missing silver: **Dining Room - chest by west wall**
H. Fingerprints on glass: **Kitchen - near sink**
I. Torn pillow: **Study - floor near door**
J. Missing jewels: **Bedroom - vanity on east wall**
K. Broken pot: **Patio - floor**
L. Cracked mirror: **Powder Room - east wall**
M. Broken window: **Bedroom - north wall**
Place 5 more mysterious clues in the house. Write the name, location and position of each.
1. **Answers will vary.**
2.
3.
4.
5.

Page 59

Page 60

Listening/Following Directions   Name _____

State Secret

Follow the directions to create the names of the first and last states to officially enter the United States.

Write the word FIRST.   **FIRST**

Change the second consonant to the twelfth letter of the alphabet.   **FILST**

Change the vowel to the last vowel in STATE.   **FELST**

At the end of the word, add the first word in the compound word WAREHOUSE.   **FELSTWARE**

Cross out the letter that appears three times in CONSTITUTION.   **FELSWARE**

Change the third consonant from the end to the second vowel from the beginning of the word.   **FELAWARE**

Change the first letter to the eighth letter in INDEPENDENCE to discover the name of the first state.   **DELAWARE**

Write the word LAST.   **LAST**

Change the third letter to the fourth letter from the end of the alphabet.   **LAWT**

Cross out the third consonant.   **LAW**

Add the vowel that is found in the middle of STATE to the end of the word   **LAWA**

At the end of the word, add all of the vowels that are found in HIKING.   **LAWAII**

Change the first letter to the last letter in FIFTIETH to discover the name of the last state.   **HAWAII**

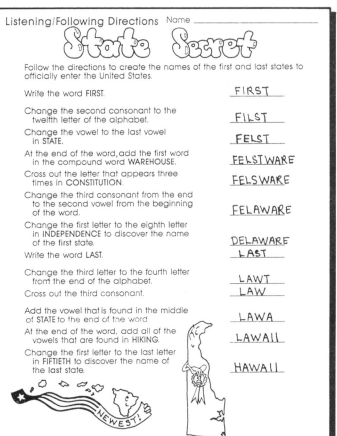

Page 60

Answer Key

Target Practice

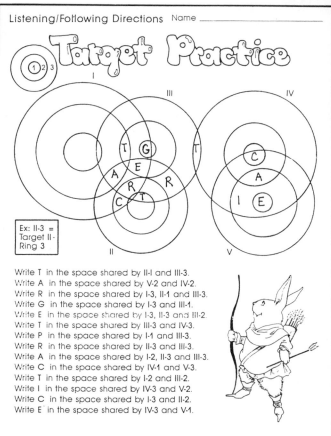

Ex: II-3 =
Target II -
Ring 3

Write T in the space shared by II-1 and III-3.
Write A in the space shared by V-2 and IV-2.
Write R in the space shared by I-3, II-1 and III-3.
Write G in the space shared by I-3 and III-1.
Write E in the space shared by I-3, II-3 and III-2.
Write T in the space shared by III-3 and IV-3.
Write P in the space shared by I-1 and III-3.
Write R in the space shared by II-3 and III-3.
Write A in the space shared by I-2, II-3 and III-3.
Write C in the space shared by IV-1 and V-3.
Write T in the space shared by I-2 and III-2.
Write I in the space shared by IV-3 and V-2.
Write C in the space shared by I-3 and II-2.
Write E in the space shared by IV-3 and V-1.

Page 61

Alphabetize to Capital-ize!

Write 1-6 to put each international city in alphabetical order.

A. (1)Beirut (2)Brasilia (4)Madrid (5)Milan (3)Lima (6)Perth
B. (6)Tokyo (2)Ottawa (1)Oslo (5)Stockholm (4)Sidney (3)Rome
C. (2)Athens (3)Bagdad (5)Cairo (1)Alexandria (4)Bonn (6)Canton
D. (4)Vienna (2)Perth (5)Warsaw (3)Venice (6)Wellington (1)Paris
E. (4)Nairobi (5)Naples (2)Mexico City (3)Moscow (6)New Delhi (1)Mecca
F. (5)Paris (6)Peking (2)Jerusalem (3)Lagos (4)London (1)Florence

Use the code of letters and numbers above to find the name of each capital.

Paris, France — F-5
London, England — F-4
Nairobi, Kenya — E-4
Brasilia, Brazil — A-2
Ottawa, Canada — B-2
Stockholm, Sweden — B-5
Bonn, Germany — C-4
Jerusalem, Israel — i-2
Madrid, Spain — A-4
Warsaw, Poland — D-5
Vienna, Austria — D-4
Cairo, Egypt — C-5
Mexico City, Mexico — E-2
Lima, Peru — A-3
Athens, Greece — C-2
Rome, Italy — B-3
New Delhi, India — E-6
Tokyo, Japan — B-6
Moscow, Russia — E-3
Wellington, New Zealand — D-8
Lagos, Nigeria — F-3

Page 62

Directionally Speaking

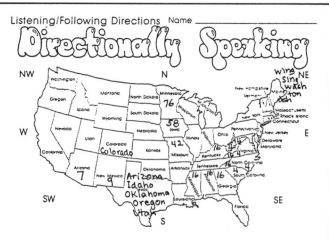

1. Traveling from northern Texas west to southern California, you would go through two states. Under each state's name, write the number of letters in each name.
2. If you stood at the southeast corner of Utah, you would touch the southwest corner of another state. Write that state's name on the state just north of New Mexico.
3. Write the number of letters in Ohio on that many states southeast of it.
4. Locate the first three states directly south of North Dakota. If A-L = 8 and M-Z = 6, add the value of each state. Write each total on the state directly east of each state.
5. Use the letters in the most northwest state (other than Alaska) to make 5 new words. Write the words just east of the most northeast state.
6. Multiply the number of E's times the number of S's and N's in the name of Tennessee. Write that number in each state that touches Tennessee to the north, east and south.
7. Find each state west of Kansas whose name begins with a vowel. Write the states' names in alphabetical order on the state southwest of Arkansas.
8. Put your initials on your state. Find any other state whose name has the same number of letters as your state. If it is northeast, east, southeast or south of your state, write your initials on it in small letters. If it is southwest, west, northwest or north, write your initials in capital letters.

Page 63

Alpha-Bet You Can Do This!

A B C D E F G H I J K L M N O P Q R S T U V W X Y Z

	1	2	3	4
1	V	R	T	L
2	H	I	C	G
3	S	N	Y	W
4	E	A	D	O

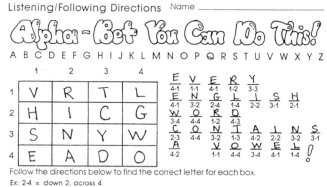

E V E R Y
4-1 1-1 4-1 1-2 3-3
E N G L I S H
4-1 3-2 2-4 1-4 2-2 3-1 2-1
W O R D
3-4 4-4 4-1 4-3
C O N T A I N S
2-3 4-4 3-2 1-3 4-2 3-2 3-1
A V O W E L!
4-2 1-1 4-4 3-4 4-1 1-4

Follow the directions below to find the correct letter for each box.

Ex: 2-4 = down 2, across 4

3-3 : Write the third letter after the twenty-second letter.
4-1 : Write the ninth letter before the eleventh consonant.
2-3 : If the alphabet were numbered 1-26, write the letter you would have for the answer to 36 ÷ 12.
1-4 : Write the letter between the eleventh and thirteenth letters.
3-4 : Write the letter that is eight letters after the next to the last vowel.
2-1 : Write the letter that comes between the third vowel and the seventeenth consonant from the end.
1-2 : If you start with A and count every other letter, write the letter which comes between the ninth and tenth letters.
4-3 : Skipping all vowels, write the letter which comes nineteenth from the end of the alphabet.
1-1 : Write the sixth consonant after the fourth vowel.
3-2 : Write the letter which comes between the tenth consonant and the second vowel from the end.
4-2 : Write the letter which comes just before the twenty-first consonant from the end.
2-4 : If the alphabet were numbered 1-26 starting at the end, write the letter you would have for the answer to 100 ÷ 5.
3-1 : Write the ninth consonant after the third vowel.
4-4 : Skipping the first five letters, write the second letter after the seventh consonant.
1-3 : Write the fifth consonant after the fourth vowel.
2-2 : Write the nearest vowel to the ninteenth letter from the end.
• Now, write the correct letter on each line to find the answer to the puzzle.

Page 64

Page 65

Listening/Following Directions   Name _____

Know Thyself!

One Great Kid!

Write 1-6 to alphabetize the words in each line. Write the fifth word in alphabetical order on the correct lines below. Complete each answer.

A. ④signal ③sign ⑤signature ⑥silence ①sift ②sight
B. ⑥ceremony ③centipede ②cent ⑤century ①cement ④central
C. ④pastei ⑤pastime ①past ③paste ②pasta ⑥pastry
D. ⑤graduate ②graceful ③gracious ⑥grain ①grab ④grade
E. ⑥charades ④chapter ②chant ①channel ⑤characteristics ③chap
F. ③tailor ⑤talents ①tactic ④tailspin ⑥talk ②taffy
G. ④wayside ②wavy ⑤weakness ⑥wealth ③way ①wattage
H. ③forecast ⑥forest ④forego ②forceful ⑤foreign ①football
I. ③amateur ⑤ambition ②amass ⑥amble ①always ④amazing
J. ⑤admire ④admiral ①adept ③adjust ②adjective ⑥admit

1. The person whom I most **admire** is _____. (J)
2. My **signature** is _____. (A)
3. My **ambition** is to be a _____. (I)
4. At the turn of the next **century**, I will be _____ years old. (B)
5. My favorite **pastime** is _____. (C)
6. I will **graduate** from high school in the year _____. (D)
7. My worst **weakness** is _____. (G)
8. My best **characteristics** are _____. (E)
9. My **talents** are _____. (F)
10. The **foreign** country I most want to visit is _____. (H)

Page 66

Listening/Following Directions   Name _____

Size 'em Up!

Write C on the left leg of the second tallest boy.
Write Y between the third tallest girl and the second tallest boy.
Write L above the shortest boy.
Write A on the third tallest boy's right hand.
Write S on the tallest boy's left ear.
Write O between the two people closest to the third tallest boy.
Write E on the shirt of the person between the second tallest boy and the shortest boy.
Write T above the third person from the tallest boy.
Write P on right shoe of the third tallest girl.
Write H between the two people between the third tallest girl and the shortest boy.
Write I on the face of the third tallest person.
Write M above the second shortest person.

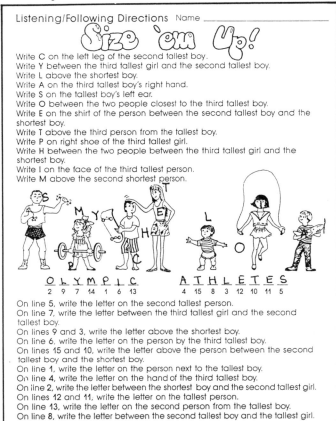

O L Y M P I C   A T H L E T E S
2 9 7 14 1 6 13   8 3 12 10 11 5

On line 5, write the letter on the second tallest person.
On line 7, write the letter between the third tallest girl and the second tallest boy.
On lines 9 and 3, write the letter above the shortest boy.
On line 6, write the letter on the person by the third tallest boy.
On lines 15 and 10, write the letter above the person between the second tallest boy and the shortest boy.
On line 1, write the letter on the person next to the tallest boy.
On line 4, write the letter on the hand of the third tallest boy.
On line 2, write the letter between the shortest boy and the second tallest girl.
On lines 12 and 11, write the letter on the tallest person.
On line 13, write the letter on the second person from the tallest boy.
On line 8, write the letter between the second tallest boy and the tallest girl.
On line 14, write the letter above the second shortest person.

Page 67

Sequencing   Name _____

In Order, Ole!

Read the recipe carefully. Write 1-15 in the circles to put the cooking steps in the correct order.

Tantalizing Tacos

In a large skillet, melt a tablespoon of butter over medium heat. Sauté 1/2 cup of chopped onions. Add a pound of ground beef and cook until brown. Add one eight-ounce can of tomato sauce. Add 1/4 teaspoon of chili powder. Add 1/4 teaspoon of salt. Add 1/4 teaspoon of garlic salt. Stir the seasoned meat mixture well and cook over low heat for 15 minutes.

While the meat mixture cooks, shred a pound of cheese. Chop a small jar of green olives. Chop 3 tomatoes and 1/2 a head of lettuce. Chop one bunch of green onions.

Heat 10 taco shells. Fill each half-full with meat mixture. On top, add cheese, lettuce, tomatoes, olives and onions.

- ⑪ Chop 3 tomatoes and 1/2 a head of lettuce.
- ⑥ Add 1/4 teaspoon of salt.
- ① In a skillet, melt a tablespoon of butter over medium heat.
- ⑫ Chop a bunch of green onions.
- ⑧ Stir well and cook over low heat for 15 minutes.
- ④ Add one eight-ounce can of tomato sauce.
- ⑮ On top, add cheese, lettuce, tomatoes, olives and onions.
- ⑦ Add 1/4 teaspoon of garlic salt.
- ③ Add a pound of ground beef and cook until brown.
- ⑬ Heat 10 taco shells.
- ⑤ Add 1/4 teaspoon of chili powder.
- ② Sauté 1/2 cup of chopped onions.
- ⑩ Chop a small jar of green olives.
- ⑭ Fill taco shells half-full with meat mixture.
- ⑨ While the meat mixture cooks, shred a pound of cheese.

Page 68

Sequencing   Name _____

To Become a Citizen...

If you were born in the U.S. or born to citizens of the U.S., you are automatically a citizen of the U.S. If you are not a citizen and desire to become one, you must follow this procedure. First, you must obtain an application form, fingerprint card and biographical information form from the Immigration and Naturalization Service. Next, you must complete the forms according to specific instructions. Return the forms to the Immigration and Naturalization Service. You will then be informed of an appointment date to meet an examiner to discuss your application. You must take two witnesses who are U.S. citizens to the meeting with you. After the meeting, you must wait at least 30 days before a final hearing in court. At the hearing, you may be asked questions about the U.S. If the court decides you can become a citizen, you must take an Oath of Allegiance to the U.S.

☆ Rewrite the sentences on the lines to put the steps in order.

- Return the forms to the Immigration and Naturalization Service.
- At the hearing, you may be asked questions about the U.S.
- Take two witnesses who are U.S. citizens to the meeting with you.
- Obtain an application form, fingerprint card and biographical information form.
- You must take an Oath of Allegiance to the U.S.
- You must wait at least 30 days before a final hearing in court.
- Complete the forms according to specific instructions.
- The court will make a decision about your application.
- You will be informed of an appointment date to discuss your application.

1. Obtain an application form, fingerprint card and biographical information form.
2. Complete the forms according to specific instructions.
3. Return the forms to the Immigration and Naturalization Service.
4. You will be informed of an appointment date to discuss your application.
5. Take two witnesses who are U.S. citizens to the meeting with you.
6. You must wait at least 30 days before a final hearing in court.
7. At the hearing, you may be asked questions about the U.S.
8. The court will make a decision about your application.
9. You must take an Oath of Allegiance to the U.S.

Answer Key

Sequencing   Name _____

A. B. C.

B.C. dates are counted backwards, unlike our present-day dates which are counted forward.
   Ex. The year 3500 BC. came before the year 858. Read the list of B.C. events. Write 1 – 19 to put the events in sequence from the earliest to the most recent.

- **10** Homer writes the Iliad in 800 B.C.
- **7** In 1750 BC., Hammurabi's Code was accepted.
- **16** The Appian Way was built in 312 BC.
- **8** In 1500 BC., iron was discovered.
- **11** The Olympic Games began in 776 BC.
- **1** In 4000 BC., the horse was domesticated.
- **13** The Babylonian Empire fell in 539 BC.
- **12** In 650 BC., coins were invented.
- **19** The Julian Calendar was established in 45 BC.
- **2** In 3600 BC., a form of writing was first used.
- **9** The transmission of the alphabet occurred in 1250 BC.
- **4** In 3300 BC., bronze was invented.
- **17** Geometry was formally developed in 300 BC.
- **6** In 2400 BC., the camel was domesticated.
- **14** The Persians invaded Greece in 470 BC.
- **5** In 2550 BC., the Great Pyramid was built.
- **18** Caesar conquered Gaul in 58 BC.
- **3** In 3500 BC., the wheel was used.
- **15** The Parthenon was built in 447 BC.

Name two events from above that occurred before Homer wrote the Iliad.
1. Answers will vary.
2. _____

Name two events from above that occurred after the Persians invaded Greece.
1. _____
2. _____

Sequencing   Name _____

A Shift in Time

Read each sentence about two events. One event should happen first and the other event second. Write each event on the correct line.

1. The day after school was out for the summer, Kim and her family moved to Texas.
   First: The day after school was out for the summer
   Second: Kim and her family moved to Texas

2. Before leaving for work, Mrs. Harris scraped ice and snow from the windshield.
   First: Mrs. Harris scraped ice and snow from the windshield
   Second: Before leaving for work

3. Pat's class is planning a trip to the capital when they graduate from junior high.
   First: When they graduate from junior high
   Second: Pat's class is planning a trip to the capital

4. Craig worked hard all summer to earn enough money to buy a new bike.
   First: Craig worked hard all summer
   Second: to earn enough money to buy a new bike

5. The landscapers dug and mulched the gardens before planting seeds for new flowers.
   First: The landscapers dug and mulched the gardens
   Second: before planting seeds for new flowers

6. Before continuing his speech, the speaker sipped water and cleared his throat.
   First: the speaker sipped water and cleared his throat
   Second: Before continuing his speech

Sequencing   Name _____

Freedom Facts

Read each event in the Revolutionary War. Write each event in the correct order under the correct heading.

Sept. 23, 1779 — John Paul Jones captured British ship "Serapis."
Apr. 19, 1775 — Minutemen fought Redcoats at Lexington and Concord.
Jan. 3, 1777 — Washington gained victory at Princeton.
Dec. 4, 1782 — The British left Charleston.
Oct. 7, 1780 — American frontiersmen stormed the British on King's Mountain.
Mar. 7, 1776 — The British evacuated Boston.
Oct. 19, 1781 — Cornwallis' forces surrendered at Yorktown.
July 3, 1775 — Washington becomes commander of Continental Army.
Dec. 19, 1777 — Washington's men began their winter at Valley Forge.
Sept. 3, 1783 — U.S. and England sign final peace treaty.
Feb. 6, 1778 — U.S. and France become allies.
June 17, 1775 — British troops win the Battle of Bunker Hill.
July 11, 1782 — The British evacuated Savannah.
Sept. 15, 1776 — The British occupied New York City.
Dec. 29, 1778 — The Redcoats entered Savannah.

Revolutionary War Highlights

1775 – 1776
April 19, 1775: Minutemen fought Redcoats at Lexington and Concord.
June 17, 1775: British troops win the Battle of Bunker Hill.
July 3, 1775: Washington becomes commander of Continental Army.
Mar. 7, 1776: The British evacuated Boston.
Sept. 15, 1776: The British occupied New York City.

1777 – 1779
Jan. 3, 1777: Washington gained victory at Princeton.
Dec. 19, 1777: Washington's men began their winter at Valley Forge.
Feb. 6, 1778: U.S. and France become allies.
Dec. 29, 1778: The Redcoats entered Savannah.
Sept. 23, 1779: John Paul Jones captured British ship "Serapis."

1780 – 1783
Oct. 7, 1780: American frontiersmen stormed the British on King's Mountain.
Oct. 19, 1781: Cornwallis' forces surrendered at Yorktown.
July 11, 1782: The British evacuated Savannah.
Dec. 4, 1782: The British left Charleston.
Sept. 3, 1783: U.S. and England sign final peace treaty.

Sequencing   Name _____

Bestsellers

Book titles give strong clues about the contents of books. Some titles can indicate that the book deals with some kind of sequence. Ex: Ten Steps to Better Tennis

Answers will vary.

Read each sentence. Use a "sequence phrase" below to write a title for each book.

A Listing of . . .   Year to Year   Steps in . .
Through the Ages   Top Ten . . .   A Five-Step Plan . . .
A Checklist . .   Past to Present   1960 – 1980

1. This book is about kinds of music.
2. This book is about favorite desserts.
3. This book is about U.S. Presidents.
4. This book is about popular TV shows.
5. This book is about space exploration.
6. This book is about scientific discoveries.
7. This book is about training animals.
8. This book is about learning to water-ski.
9. This book is about traveling to South America.

Answer Key

©1992 Instructional Fair, Inc.   121   IF8712 Reading Skills

Sequencing   Name _____

A Matter of Time

Each sentence tells of two things that happened. The order of the events in the sentence may or may not be the order in which they happened. In each sentence:
Put one line under the event that happened first.
Put two lines under the event that happened second.
On each line, write 1-2 or 2-1 to tell the order of events in the sentence.

1. **2 1** Before mowing the yard, Paul changed to old clothes and sneakers.
2. **1 2** Just after Sarah started to shower, the phone rang.
3. **2 1** The football team was honored at a banquet after they won the championship game.
4. **2 1** By the time they had reached the theater, the movie had already begun.
5. **1 2** Shortly after the lights were dimmed, the orchestra began the concert.
6. **2 1** Before going back to camp, the hikers poured water on their campfire.
7. **1 2** The escaped prisoner was free for two days before he was captured.
8. **1 2** After visiting several animal hospitals, Kevin decided to become a veterinarian.
9. **2 1** The museum exhibit was flown to Paris at the end of its New York show.
10. **1 2** The spectators ran indoors just before the thunderstorm began.

On the lines below, write four sentences, each with two events in the following order:

1 - 2 _____
2 - 1 _____
1 - 2 _____
2 - 1 _____

Page 73

Sequencing   Name _____

Washington Lifenotes

Below is a list of highlights of George Washington's life. Write 1 – 18 on the lines to put the events in order.

George Washington

12 Oct. 19, 1781 : Victory at Yorktown.
15 Dec. 3, 1792 : Re-elected President of the United States.
8 Jan. 6, 1759 : Married Mrs. Martha Dandridge Curtis.
2 July 18, 1749 : Became official surveyor in Virginia.
6 July 9, 1755 : Ambushed by French and Indians.
11 June 15, 1775 : Elected Commander of Continental Army.
18 Dec. 14, 1799 : Died at Mount Vernon at age 67.
4 Oct. 28, 1753 : Carried British ultimatum to French.
1 Feb. 22, 1732 : Born in Westmoreland Country, Virginia.
17 July 4, 1798 : Became Commander of U.S. Army.
5 July 3, 1754 : Surrendered Fort Necessity in French and Indian War.
16 Sept. 19, 1796 : Published Farewell Address refusing third term.
3 Feb. 5, 1751 : Made only trip out of U.S. — to Barbados Island.
10 Mar. 4, 1775 : Elected delegate to Second Continental Congress.
14 Feb. 18, 1789 : Elected first United States President.
7 Aug. 20, 1755 : Commanded Virginia's frontier troops.
13 May 25, 1787 : Became president of Constitutional Convention.
9 Sept. 3, 1774 : Elected delegate to First Continental Congress.

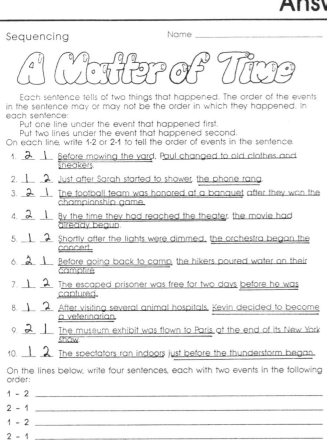

Page 74

Sequencing   Name _____

Building Blocks

Read the names of architectural styles through the ages. Write 1 – 15 to put the dates in order. (Remember: B.C. before A.D. and B.C. dates go "backwards.") Write each date by an architectural style starting from the earliest to the latest date.

1. Egyptian Pyramids **2700 B.C.**
2. China's Wooden Temples **1027 B.C.**
3. Roman Arches **27 B.C.**
4. Byzantine **400 A.D.**
5. Mayan & Aztec Temples **1100 A.D.**
6. Romanesque **1100 A.D.**
7. Gothic **1150 A.D.**
8. Renaissance **1400 A.D.**
9. Baroque **1600 A.D.**
10. Rococo **1700 A.D.**
11. Classical **1720 A.D.**
12. Romanticism **1100 A.D.**
13. Colonial **1770 A.D.**
14. Revival **1800 A.D.**
15. Organic **1920 A.D.**

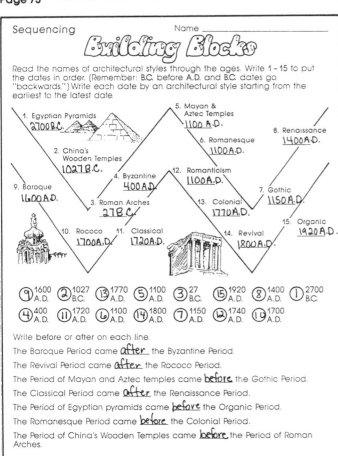

⑨1600 A.D.   ②1027 B.C.   ⑬1770 A.D.   ⑤1100 A.D.   ③27 B.C.   ⑮1920 A.D.   ⑧1400 A.D.   ①2700 B.C.
④400 A.D.   ⑪1720 A.D.   ⑥1100 A.D.   ⑭1800 A.D.   ⑦1150 A.D.   ⑫1740 A.D.   ⑩1700 A.D.

Write before or after on each line.
The Baroque Period came **after** the Byzantine Period.
The Revival Period came **after** the Rococo Period.
The Period of Mayan and Aztec temples came **before** the Gothic Period.
The Classical Period came **after** the Renaissance Period.
The Period of Egyptian pyramids came **before** the Organic Period.
The Romanesque Period came **before** the Colonial Period.
The Period of China's Wooden Temples came **before** the Period of Roman Arches.

Page 75

Sequencing   Name _____

I C TV

Probably the most popular form of entertainment, TV is a mystery to most people. Read the following paragraph which tells how a color TV works.

Color TV begins with a TV camera. A mirror separates the light from a scene into red, blue and green. A microphone changes sounds into audio signals. Camera tubes change the color light into video signals. These signals go to an encoder which makes a new color signal. A transmitter combines the audio and video signals for broadcast.
A receiver picks up the signals with an antenna. The signals move to the tuner which selects the correct station. The signals are separated into audio and video signals. The audio signals are changed into sound. The video signals are changed back to red, blue and green light. The TV screen is covered with dots of red, blue and green. The dots glow and form a color picture.

Write 1 – 13 to put the sentences in the correct order.

⑧ The signals move to the tuner which selects the correct station.
③ A microphone changes sounds into audio signals.
⑫ The TV screen is covered with dots of red, blue and green.
⑤ The signals go to an encoder which makes a new color signal.
⑬ The dots glow and form a color picture.
① Color TV begins with a TV camera.
⑪ The video signals are changed back to red, blue and green light.
⑦ A receiver picks up the signals with an antenna.
⑨ The signals are separated into audio and video signals.
④ Camera tubes change the color light into video signals.
⑩ The audio signals are changed into sounds.
② A mirror separates the light from a scene into red, blue and green.
⑥ A transmitter combines audio and video signals for broadcast.

Page 76

Answer Key

Page 77

Vocabulary   Name _____

Quick Change

The first and last word in each sequence have been given. Change only one letter at a time in the middle steps to reach the final word. Then write each middle step word in the sentence in which it belongs. The sentences are not necessarily in order.

TRACK
T R A C E
B R A C E
B R A V E
CRAVE

The settlers made friends with one Indian **brave**.

Luke found a piece of wood to act as a **brace** for the wobbly cabinet.

There was not a **trace** of any foul play in the woman's sudden death.

BLIND
B L A N D
B L A N K
P L A N K
PLANT

The cookies were **bland**, much to our disappointment.

The men put a **plank** from the steps of the new house over the muddy ditch in front of them.

Much to the teacher's surprise, Sandy turned in a **blank** piece of paper.

PORCH
P O U C H
C O U C H
C O U G H
TOUGH

The kangaroo carried the baby in its **pouch**.

After two weeks, Larry went to the doctor for his **cough**.

The dog jumped up on the family's new **couch** with a bone.

TOWEL
T O W E R
P O W E R
P O K E R
JOKER

After the storm was over, it took the **power** company several hours to fix the lights.

The ranger had to leave the **tower** when the flames came close.

Dad used a **poker** to stoke the fire.

Page 78

Vocabulary   Name _____

Analogies

Fill in the blanks with a word from the box to the left of each group.

YARD
MINUTE
AUTONOMOUS
SCRIPT
LESS
QUILL
CORE
YELLOW
NUMERALS
FLAME
UNIVERSE

Script is to play as choreography is to dance. Fence is to **yard** as border is to state. **Quill** is to stench as porcupine is to skunk. Aquarius is to Zodiac as Venus is to **universe**. **Autonomous** is to gregarious as single is to many. Flake is to **flame** as chasm is to charm. Grand is to voluminous as petite is to **minute**. Prefix is to suffix as anti is to **less**. Letters are to words as **numerals** are to numbers. **Core** is to earth as eye is to hurricane. Red is to Ned as **yellow** is to fellow.

PARAGRAPHS
PLANT
BOTANIST
ORAL
FINISH
SAILOR
DISTANCE
SCENT
CANVAS
BARE
STATE

Vocabulary is to paragraph as **paragraphs** are to books. Aural is to hearing as **oral** is to speaking. **Bare** is to bear as beat is to beet. Pen is to paper as brush is to **canvas**. Zoologist is to **botanist** as ape is to coleus. Soldier is to army as **sailor** is to navy. Time is to **distance** as hour is to mile. Quilt is to sew as **plant** is to sow. Exam is to final as end is to **finish**. **Scent** is to odor as cent is to money. County is to **state** as state is to nation.

Page 79

Vocabulary   Name _____

Explain These!

Circle the answers within the following questions.

Would you use a lariat for a trip on the river or (a cow on the range)?
Would a person who is subtle be (delicate and cunning) or boistrous and wild?
Would a patina be a (old finish) or a little bear?
Would a breach be a place to swim or (a break of contract)?
Would you use a thesaurus to look (for synonyms) or definitions of words?
Would a choreographer map out the coral reefs on the ocean floor or the (steps of a dance on the stage)?
Would cholesterol be found (in chicken eggs) or in a diamond mine?
Would a faction be a partial whole number or (a sub-group sharing like beliefs)?
Would you placate a person to (calm him down) or prepare him for surgery?
Would you see a philatelist at (a stamp show) or an outdoor show?
Would a frugal person be apt (to have the first dollar ever earned) or a tendency to get sick often?
Would you use a caladoose to (detain a criminal) or store fodder for pigs?
Would an aptitude test determine (one's ability) or agility?
Would a cartographer be knowledgeable about (meridians and parallels) or carts, cars and carriages?
Would a biased person be one who has (a prejudice) or no money?
Would you use calipers when measuring the distance between fence posts or (the thickness of a pipe)?
Would you masticate (your dinner) or your dog?
Would you extricate a criminal from jail or (a tooth for filling)?
Would a deplorable person (cheat his best friend) or study diplomacy?
Would you incarcerate a pig for market or (a man for breaking the law)?
Would you be apt to see a menagerie (at a circus) or a courthouse?
Would a tenacious person be prone to tendonitis or (stubbornness)?
Would you use a scythe to comb your hair or (cut the weeds)?
Would a neurologist (care for you) or study neutrons?

TO THE MENAGERIE

Page 80

Vocabulary   Name _____

Using Is Confusing!

Above each pair of sentences are two or three words. Write the correct word in each sentence.

lying   laying   lying

I am **laying** the book on the table.
I am **lying** about who took the book to protect him.
I am **lying** down for awhile.

beside   besides

Our cat was buried **beside** our dog in the backyard.
Besides making dessert for the church social, Mary made salad.

uninterested   disinterested

They chose a **disinterested** person to act as the referee to settle the argument.
The **uninterested** man was bored when he had to go to the ballet with his wife.

inflammable   inflammatory

Tempers flared after the **inflammatory** speech.
Be careful to select **inflammable** material when knitting the baby's sweater.

lay   laid   lied

I **laid** down yesterday for a little while.
I **lied** yesterday when I said I would go with you.
I **lay** the ornament carefully on the shelf.

biennially   biannually

Congressmen from every state are elected **biennially** to the House of Representatives in Washington.
The Science Club meets **biannually**, March first and September first, to share their findings.

amend   emend

They had to **amend** the lease by adding a clause about damage.
Before Terry typed his report, he had to **emend** it where necessary.

Answer Key

Page 81

What's What?

Above each pair of sentences are two words written with their diacritical spellings. Write the regular spelling for the two words on the line to the right of them. Then, use the diacritical spelling to write the correct word in each sentence.

proj´ ekt   prō jekt´   **project**

The speaker needs to **prō jekt´** his voice.

The Garden Club agreed to make beautifying the city their **proj´ ekt** for the year.

pra dōōs´   prō´ doos   **produce**

The **prō´ doos** at the market was spoiled.

Jim and Jerry wanted to **pra dōōs´** a play for the class.

wōōnd   wound   **wound**

The nurse bandaged Tim's **wōōnd** .

Larry **wound** the string around the gate to hold it shut.

kan tent´   kon´ tent   **content**

The boys were disappointed to find the box's **kon´ tent** was nothing but broken glass.

The boys were **kan tent´** to stay inside and watch television when it started to rain.

min´ it   mī nōōt´   **minute**

There was a **mī nōōt´** piece of dirt on the camera lens.

In just a **min´ it** the bell will ring for third period.

in val´ ad   in´ va lid   **invalid**

The results of the race were **in val´ ad** because the timer started his watch late.

The results of the medical tests showed that Gramps would soon be an **in´ va lid** .

wīnd   wind   **wind**

Debris flew everywhere when the **wind** kicked up.

Hank forgot to **wīnd** his alarm, and so he was late for work.

Page 82

Brains Speak!

Begin where the arrow is pointing. Decode the message clockwise in each brain. Then write a reply from the "speaker's" mouth.

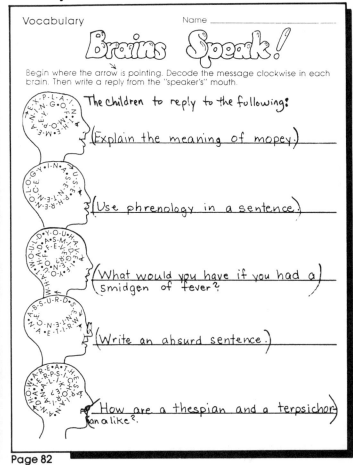

The children to reply to the following:

(Explain the meaning of mopey.) _____

(Use phrenology in a sentence.) _____

(What would you have if you had a) smidgen of fever? _____

(Write an absurd sentence.) _____

(How are a thespian and a terpsichor an alike?) _____

Page 83

There's Truth to This!

Color the conjunctions yellow, the prepositions blue and the adverbs green. Find a message about you.

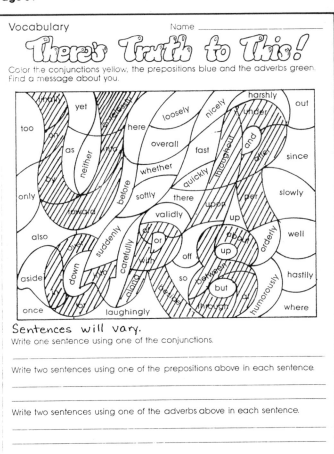

Sentences will vary.

Write one sentence using one of the conjunctions.

_____

Write two sentences using one of the prepositions above in each sentence.

_____
_____

Write two sentences using one of the adverbs above in each sentence.

_____
_____

Page 84

Scrambled Modifiers

Unscramble the adjectives below.

hiteg	**eight**	ilaeg	**agile**
ilvjoa	**jovial**	glines	**single**
ourasougec	**courageous**	lemwol	**mellow**
edergy	**greedy**	kicdew	**wicked**
udends	**sudden**	ngnaul	**annual**
cenedt	**decent**	velloy	**lovely**
nugoy	**young**	lnamyren	**mannerly**
itctatarve	**attractive**	gridif	**frigid**

Unscramble the adverbs below.

bofree	**before**	fyeblauulti	**beautifully**
tanyle	**neatly**	sisbeed	**besides**
veabo	**above**	woeritshe	**otherwise**
oorlyhguht	**thoroughly**	tlasom	**almost**
tyslfo	**softly**	sdmoel	**seldom**
yislae	**easily**	rlyrdhuei	**hurriedly**
tqleuyi	**quietly**	sslyineb	**sensibly**
cehwne	**whence**	lgneyt	**gently**

Use a word from above that will make sense in the sentences below.

Jason acted **sensibly** when he lost his **single** house key.

Wendy saw the **courageous** team **before** they lost the **annual** game.

The cookies were hidden **above** the refrigerator.

Eight **young** racers ran into each other when they hit a bump.

Everyone **thoroughly** enjoyed the movie.

Frank **easily** turns his work in on time.

When you pet a newborn pet, handle it **gently** .

Who else is going **besides** the three boys?

They **hurriedly** cut the grass so they could play ball.

The **lovely** music was playing **softly** .

Answer Key

Page 85

Next of Kin

Circle two or three words in each parenthesis which are related in some way to the word on the left.

kin (ancestors) (relatives) (descendents) ascends friend)
flower (rapid (petal) tall pedal (stem))
barrel (race) final (stave) witch (rainwater))
finances (account) school spirit weather (taxes))
medical (linotype (scalpel) (sutures) (prescription) marble)
performer (roll (theater) (script) companion (role))
compass (plate (direction) (needle) spider quantity)
bone (calcium) harmful (tibia) phonetic vegetation)
desert (forest (sandy) (arid) zebras equator)
instrument (microscope) chorus (calliope) (surgeon) (axe))
infant (toddler) (carriage) (lullaby) chemical longitude)
tackle (reel) (football) (bridle) ocean psychotic)
equipment (manpower (paraphernalia) vintage (accoutrement))
tripod (telescope) (photography) (transit) tricycle peas)
religious (pious) (cathedral) sensitive fastidious alter)
military (platoon) (maneuvers) (armory) dresser prison)

Use some of the circled words from above to complete the sentences below.

1. Milk has a lot of __calcium__ in it.
2. The pharmacist filled the __prescription__ quickly.
3. Every Saturday the __armory__ serves as a center for the military.
4. The climate was hot and __arid__.
5. He packed all the __paraphernalia__ necessary to do the job.
6. The __needle__ wavered three degrees.
7. The preacher was a __pious__ man.
8. The surveyor set up his __transit__ to prepare for the new highway.
9. The __barrel__ was warped.
10. When the merry-go-round went around, the __calliope__ played.
11. The director of the drama interpreted the __script__ for the actors.

Page 86

Reptiles

Read the following paragraphs. Then follow the directions below.

Reptiles are cold-blooded animals with dry, scaly skin. They are vertebrates that breathe by means of lungs. Lizards and snakes make up the largest group of reptiles. There are about 3,000 species of each. Turtles are the only reptiles with shells. There are about 240 different kinds of turtles. Alligators, caymans, crocodiles and gavials belong to the crocodilian group of which there are about 20 species. Reptiles live all over the world (except Antarctica) except for the last group, the tuatara, which lives only on the New Zealand coast.

Reptiles evolved from amphibians which lived near water so their eggs would be kept moist. Reptiles developed eggs that would hold moisture, and then they were able to live away from water. Dinosaurs were reptiles and were the dominant animals during the Age of Reptiles, 65-225 million years ago. Scientists do not know for sure why dinosaurs disappeared, but their descendents may be in danger of becoming extinct today.

Circle the words in the puzzle you are told to find. They may be forward, backward, up, down or diagonal. Write each word after its direction.

Find the word that tells:
Reptiles have backbones. __vertebrate__

That reptiles' body temperatures stay about the same as their surroundings:
cold- __blooded__

Type or kind. __species__
That dinosaurs developed slowly. __evolved__
The name of animal that lived on land and in water. __amphibian__

Primary or main. __dominant__

How reptiles feel to touch. __dry__
The names of three descendents of
dinosaurs. __crocodile__ __lizard__ __alligator__

Do you think reptiles today could become extinct? _____ Why? _____

```
V E R F O U Y G I L L A
E V O L V E D O V L E S
A U E V I G A V I K C N
R A T R A Z I C A O R A
T E R A T E A O L T O I
S P E C I E S L U E C B
D E D O O L B D O C O D
D R A Z I L K R R R D I
A T A U O S A Q A U I L
T A R O F A N A U L H P
Y P D O M I N A N T E M
R E L Y R A U T K A T A
D R A D N A I B I P M A
```

Page 87

Natural Resources

The dwindling supply of some of America's resources has led concerned environmentalists to call for the recycling of wastes. Recycling is the process of recovering used materials, separating them from non-usable wastes, and sending them to manufacturers who make them into usable products. There are many recycling centers throughout the country. Often scouts or school programs have campaigns to gather waste materials.

Most common among recycled wastes are newspapers, aluminum and steel cans, and glass bottles. They provide material for several usable products and, at the same time, save our natural resources.

Paper comes from trees. Containers are made from minerals from the earth. Not only do manufacturers use up natural resources when they lumber or mine for these products, but they add to environmental pollution.

Answers will vary.

What natural resources are being conserved with recycling? __trees, minerals__

What could happen to animal and plant life if all natural resources disappeared? _____

What might non-usable wastes be? _____
Of what help is recycling? _____

What products might waste materials become? _____

Which Path to Take?

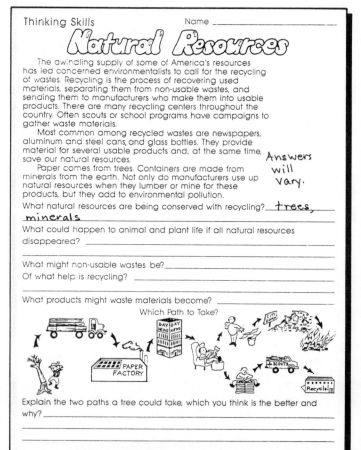

Explain the two paths a tree could take, which you think is the better and why? _____

Page 88

See the Poes Grow!

Mr. and Mrs. Poe had five children. They kept a growing chart for each child from birth to age twelve. Read the graph below and answer the questions beneath it.

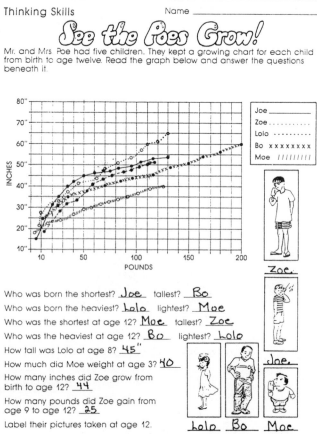

Who was born the shortest? __Joe__ tallest? __Bo__
Who was born the heaviest? __Lolo__ lightest? __Moe__
Who was the shortest at age 12? __Moe__ tallest? __Zoe__
Who was the heaviest at age 12? __Bo__ lightest? __Lolo__
How tall was Lolo at age 8? __45"__
How much did Moe weight at age 3? __40__
How many inches did Zoe grow from birth to age 12? __44__
How many pounds did Zoe gain from age 9 to age 12? __25__
Label their pictures taken at age 12.

©1992 Instructional Fair, Inc.   124   IF8712 Reading Skills

Answer Key

Thinking Skills — Truth or Fantasy?

Name _____

Write a T in front of each statement below if it is true.
Write an F in front of each statement below if it is fantasy. If you are in doubt, look the subject up. When you have finished marking the statements, color the numbers of the TRUE statements in the puzzle below red, and the numbers of the FANTASY statements orange to make a fantasy picture.

- F 1. Dr. Doolittle took care of the animals.
- T 2. Women thought to be witches were persecuted in America's early settlement days.
- T 3. Harry Houdini was an escape artist who could free himself from a nailed crate.
- F 4. John Henry was a steel-driving man who died with a hammer in his hand.
- F 5. A unicorn is a horse with a horn.
- T 6. The teddy bear was named for President T. R. Roosevelt after he refused to shoot a baby cub.
- F 7. Mike Fink was the greatest riverman on the Mississippi.
- F 8. Pecos Bill was a cowboy who invented many cowboy skills and was the first to throw a lariat.
- F 9. Tom Sawyer got all his friends to paint his fence.
- T 10. Trees usually blossom before they bear fruit.
- F 11. George Washington chopped down a cherry tree and could not tell a lie.
- F 12. Orion was a great Greek hunter.
- F 13. Snoopy is a human-acting beagle that hangs around with Lucy and Charlie Brown.
- T 14. The boll weevil is a beetle that feeds on cotton plants.
- T 15. Davy Crockett was a famous frontiersman.
- F 16. Dorothy traveled down the yellow brick road.
- T 17. Laika, a Russian dog, was the first animal to orbit Earth.
- F 18. Johnny Appleseed gave apple seeds away to early American settlers.

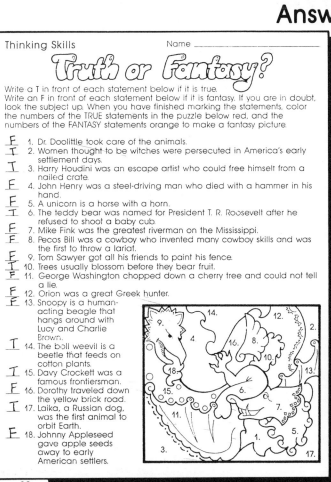

Page 89

Thinking Skills — Funny Papers

Name _____

Look at the "comic strips" below. Each one tells an incomplete story. Complete it in the last box of each strip. Then, below the strip, write an ending for the story. **Answers will vary.**

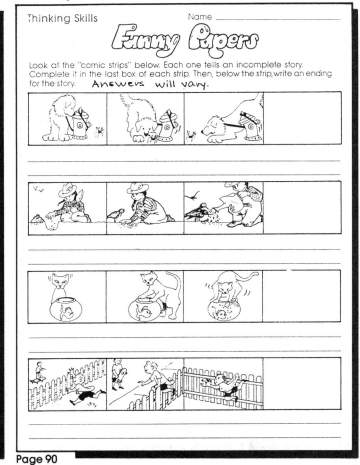

Page 90

Thinking Skills — Who or What Am I?

Name _____

Write what each paragraph is describing under it (1) and what clue gave it away (2). You can find the answers in the puzzle below. The answers appear in a running order, but not necessarily in a straight line. They may run up or down, back and forth or criss-cross. See the example to the right.

```
  3
'D O M H
 F G R C    1. dog
 A E R E    2. father
 T H Y C 4. 3. mice
                4. cry
```

I was once the political head of a country. I helped lead my country to victory in World War II. I met with Stalin and Roosevelt.

1. I am Winston Churchill
2. meeting with Stalin and Roosevelt

I am a state. My climate is usually dry. I have mountains and deserts. I was one of the last four states admitted to the Union. The first capital of the U.S. was located in me under Spanish rule.

1. I am New Mexico
2. first capital of U.S. under Spanish rule

As early as the 1400 and 1500's, some of my countrymen walked on U.S. land. They traveled a long way to get here. I am on the Iberian peninsula. My western and southern borders are on the Atlantic Ocean. Spain borders me to the north and east.

1. I am Portugal
2. Spain bordering on north and east

Answers will vary.

I like to swim. I have lungs and must come to the surface sometimes to breathe. I am a mammal and give birth to live young. The tail of a fish is vertical. Mine is horizontal.

1. I am a whale
2. mammal that swims, has lungs

I was President of the U.S. I ran for the presidency but was defeated. I lost to Jimmy Carter.

1. I am Gerald Ford
2. defeated by Jimmy Carter

I have to study a long time to do what I do. I am especially good at drawing and arithmetic. People come to me to design new products and structures. I look for better ways of using existing resources and developing new materials.

1. I am an engineer
2. designer of new products and structures

I can live a long time if conditions are right. I am the oldest known living thing. I am the largest of all plants.

1. I am a tree
2. largest of all plants

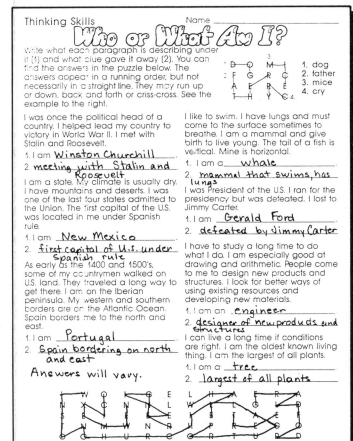

Page 91

Thinking Skills — You Name It!

Name _____

_____

Read the following paragraphs and answer the questions after them.

In 1821, William Becknell led the first wagon train from Franklin, Missouri, to Santa Fe, New Mexico. It was not easy. This was the beginning of a trade route, called the Santa Fe Trail, that was to last for fifty years.

The only outsiders the Indians of the West had known until the start of the trail had been the Spanish. The Indians had learned about horses and metal from the Spanish. The relations between the two were not always friendly, but the Indians liked some of their goods and adapted them to their lifestyle. When the wagon trains began crossing the prairies, the relationship between the Indians and the "Easterners" was somewhat the same. Some welcomed the goods being brought for trade. Some felt the arrival of the wagon trains was an invasion of their lands.

Forts were built along the Trail to protect the growing trade and passenger route and the many men who were brought to build the railroad. Soon after the railroad began service, the Santa Fe Trail ceased to operate.

Name three hardships you think the people on the wagon trains may have encountered. **Answers will vary.**

_____

What do you think some of the goods were that the wagon trains carried west? _____

With what goods do you think the wagon trains returned to the east? _____

After the railroad was in operation, would you have traveled west on the Santa Fe Trail or on the train? _____ Why? _____

Why do you think the Santa Fe Trail stopped operating? _____

Write a title for this article above it on the line at the top of the page.

Page 92

Answer Key

Thinking Skills — Name

Hat's, Etc.

First read the article about "Hats, Etc." without filling in any of the blanks. Read it again. Think about what word would make sense in each blank. Select a word from the box beneath the article. Write it where it belongs.

A hat is the **name** given to a piece of **of** clothing worn on the head. A hat has a crown **and** a **brim**. Other head **coverings** such as hoods, bonnets, and caps have no **form**, but will be considered **hats** in this article.

People wear hats for **different** reasons. One is **for** protection. They may protect the wearer **from** the climate or from bodily injury. Cowboys **wear** hats to keep cool and **football** players wear helmets to **keep** from injuring themselves. Some **forms** of headgear signal the **wearer's** profession or position. A **graduate** from high school wears a **cap** with a tassel. **An** Eskimo's hood tells he **comes** from a cold climate. The **construction** worker's helmet signals his **type** of work. The third **reason** for wearing a hat **is** appearance. Ladies like to **make** themselves attractive. Men may wear hats **to** business appointments.

No one knows exactly **how** or why hats developed, but **they** have been a part of **our** culture for millions of years.

A	form	brim	name	from	coverings	graduate	and
football	forms	cap	type	make	wearer's	An	how
they	for	our	is	to	reason	of	hats
different	comes	construction	wear	keep			

Tell who might wear the hats below and why.

Answers will vary. _____

Thinking Skills — Name

Prehistoric Transportation

First read the article about "Prehistoric Transportation" without filling in any of the blanks. Read it again. This time, think about what letters would fit in the blanks and make sense. Write them in where they belong.

Prehistoric times probably were from about 5,000,000 years ago until around 3000 B.C. Transportation, as we think of it, probably did not begin until around 10,000 BC.

In the beginning, there were not domesti**c**ated animals, w**h**eels or roads. People w**a**lked. When they t**r**aveled, everyth**i**ng they wanted t**o** carry was s**t**rapped onto their bodie**s**. If it was too heavy, it was strapped to a pole and two people c**a**rried the pole. F**r**om t**h**i**s** developed t**he** sledge which could be **a**ttached to a person and dra**g**ged along the ground be**h**ind the pers**o**n. R**unners** w**e**re ad**d**ed to the sledge in late pr**e**historic times.

By **a**bout 8000 B.C., the donkey and ox **w**ere domesticated a**n**d were us**e**d for farm work. Be**t**ween 3000-4500 years late**r**, th**e** animals w**e**re used as pack animals and harnesses were inven**t**ed so the animals **c**ould pull sledges **a**s humans had done befo**r**e them. Animal**s** could tr**a**nsport heav**i**e**r** load**s**.

With the format**i**on of communities, the need for better trans**p**ortation developed. Raft**s**, dugou**t**s and cano**e**s were invented **a**round this t**i**m**e** for use on inland s**t**r**e**ams and l**a**kes. Oars and poles were used to move them **i**n w**a**ter.

The f**i**r**s**t vehic**l**es w**i**th wheels were inve**n**t**e**d in Mesopotamia a**r**ound 3500 BC. The Egyptians invented s**a**ilboats arou**n**d 3200 BC. Wi**t**h these inventi**o**n**s**, transportation developed eventually to what we know today.

Write the letters used as fill-ins above in order to spell the names of eight vehicles that developed throughout time. Write the names below. (Some vehicles are more than one word.)

chariots cart stage horsedrawn streetcars airship steam train airliner autos

---

Thinking Skills — Name

What's For Sure?

Write an F in front of each statement below if it is a fact.
Write an O in front of each statement if it is an opinion.

F 1. Fel(i)x Mendelssohn (f)irst played the piano in public when he was ten.
O 2. The Republicans in Congress usuall(y) are better politicians than the Dem(o)crats.
O 3. Dwight Goodin is tho(u)ght to be one of baseball's finest players.
F 4. Rhode Island was the thirteenth state (i)n 1790.
O 5. Many people think the Presi(d)ent is doing a good job.
F 6. Marsupials are mammals tha(t) give birth to underdeveloped young.
O 7. Food cooked in tinfoil may not b(e) healthy.
F 8. Cyrus McCormick (i)nvented (t)he reaper.
F 9. Labor Day is always observed on the (f)irst Monday of (S)eptember.
O 10. Rock mu(s)ic has a strong b(e)at and is usually loud.
F 11. Abraham Lincoln was (a)ssassinated at Ford's Theater.
O 12. Tige(r)s are like little kittens; they are so cute.
F 13. Queen Victoria ruled England longer (t)han any other monarch.
F 14. There are more (D)emocrats in the House of Representatives than Republicans.
O 15. The opera, "Porgy and Bess," is the best American opera e(v)er writt(e)n.
F 16. Robert Da(w)son has written many books for young readers.
O 17. H(a)waii is the most beautiful of all the states.
F 18. New York Cit(y) has the largest p(o)pulation of all American cities.
F 19. The Amazon River is the longest river in the world.
O 20. The blossom(s) seem (t)o be later this yea(r) than last yea(r).
F 21. The land west of the Mississippi River covers a gre(a)ter area, but has fewer people living in it, than the area of land ea(s)t of the Mississippi in the United States.
F 22. It is n(o)t safe to fix wires in an electrical appliance while it is still plugged into a live so(c)ket.

The circled letters in the opinion statements spell out a fact about you. What is it? (4 words) **You deserve a star.**

Thinking Skills — Name

He Likes Me, He Likes Me Not!

Below are several sets of likes and dislikes. Figure out what it is in each set that makes the first part likeable and the second part not. After each set, write what the difference is between the likes and dislikes.

Mary likes cardinals, but she does not like blue jays.
Mary likes tomatoes, but she does not like squash.
Mary likes blood, but she does not like saliva.
Mary likes strawberries, but she does not like boysenberries.
The first set is red.

Harry likes a drum, but he does not like a clarinet.
Harry likes basketballs, but he does not like footballs.
Harry likes pennies, but he does not like dollars.
Harry likes to ride a ferris wheel, but he does not like to ride a roller coaster.
The first set is round.

Gayle likes marching bands, but she does not like rubber bands.
Gayle likes flashy cars, but she does not like pickup trucks.
Gayle likes to play darts, but she does not like to play pool.
Gayle likes a warm dinner, but she does not like hot drinks.
The first set has the ar sound.

Babies like beards, but they do not like eyeglasses.
Babies like monkeys, but they do not like penguins.
Babies like gerbils, but they do not like whales.
Babies like tarantulas, but they do not like roaches.
The first set is furry.

Everyone likes George, but no one likes Gary.
Everyone likes Robert, but no one likes Richard.
Everyone likes Jeanne, not no one likes Janet.
Everyone likes Merideth, but no one likes Martha.
The first set comes later in alphabetical order.

Now make up a like-dislike set of your own. See if a friend or your teacher can figure it out.

_____
_____
_____
_____

Answer Key

©1992 Instructional Fair, Inc.

Page 97

Thinking Skills   Name _____

Marble

Read the following article and answer the questions below.

Marble is a type of metamorphic rock formed from limestone. This type of rock was formed millions of years ago. Heat and pressure in the Earth's crust caused the limestone to undergo changes. This process is called recrystallization.

Impurities in the limestone, plus the temperature at the time of the crystallization, affected the mineral composition of the marble. A greater quantity of quartz resulted when the temperature was low. At higher temperatures, rarer minerals may have been produced. At times when all impurities reacted together, garnet, a precious stone, may have been formed in the marble.

The presence of minerals in greater or lesser amounts is what gives marble its color. The purest calcite marble is white. Hematite gives marble a reddish color. Marble with limonite is yellow, and marble with serpentine is green.

Marble is found in many places around the world. Georgia mines more marble than any other state. It is a strong rock that polishes well and resists weathering. It is very difficult to mine.

1. For what do you think marble is used? __*Accept reasonable answers.*__
_____

2. Why do you think it is used for these purposes? _____
_____

3. Do you think marble formed at high or low temperatures is more valuable? _____ Why? _____
_____

4. From what natural resource does marble come? _____

5. Following are some well-known structures made of marble. Unscramble the letters to find out what they are.

nasiWnthgo tmMneout __Washington Monument__

naroPetnh __Parthenon__   gWneid riVcyto __Winged Victory__

niLnloc loieaMrm __Lincoln Memorial__

ajT aahIM __Taj Mahal__ enngiLa wrToe fo iPas __Leaning Tower of Pisa__

Page 98

Thinking Skills   Name _____

If You Were Asked....

If you were asked or told to do the following, tell what would be the first thing you would do or ask? __*Accept reasonable answers.*__

1. Prepare meat loaf for dinner. _____
2. Take the dog for a walk. _____
3. Go to the store for mother. _____
4. Write a report about weather in Chile. _____
5. To be at school by 7:30 _____
6. Come home alone after school. _____
7. Call a taxi. _____
8. Get ready to go to a party. _____
9. Shelve books for the librarian. _____
10. To be a patrol person _____
11. R.S.V.P. _____
12. Fix a leaky faucet. _____
13. Prepare lettuce for a salad. _____
14. Sign for a C.O.D. package. _____
15. Baby-sit a neighbor's child. _____
16. Plan a trip to _____ (Name it.)
17. to go to a friend's after school. _____
18. Earn some money. _____
19. Use a pay phone. _____
20. Plan a camping trip. _____
21. Walk in the dark through the woods. _____
22. Save money. _____
23. Take attendance. _____
24. Help a friend find a lost wallet. _____
25. Conserve energy. _____
26. Respond to a cry of "Help!" _____
27. Buy a present for a friend. _____
28. Cut material to make a tablecloth. _____

Page 99

Thinking Skills   Name _____

Give Them a Name!

Read each paragraph below. Give each one a title on the line above it.

__Lacrosse__

Lacrosse was first played by American Indians. It is a game played with a ball and a stick that has a net pocket at one end. The object of the game is to score goals by throwing or kicking the ball into the opposing team's goal.

__Marble Terms__

Marble players have their own vocabulary. Players who shoot marbles use a "shooter" to score points by hitting "object" marbles. Usually when they shoot, players "knuckle down." Some kinds of marbles have slang names such as "glassies" and "steelies."

__Polo Ponies__

Horses used in the game of polo are called polo ponies. They are small as one might think when hearing the word "pony." Polo ponies must be fast and strong and must get used to clubs swinging overhead and being bumped by other horses upon their rider's commands. Training a pony is hard work and takes about a year.

__Card Games__

Hundreds of games can be played with cards. Solitaire is played alone. Fish and Hearts can be played with two or more players. Poker can be played with as many as ten.

__Possible titles__

__Kinds of Racing__

There are many kinds of contests of speed. Dog racing has been a sport since ancient times. Horses compete in trotting, pacing and running races. Automobile racing has occurred almost since the first car rolled off the assembly line. Boating, swimming and flying are some other racing forms.

__Baseball Equipment__

Besides the bats and balls used in a baseball game, each player has his own equipment. Every player wears a uniform with a number on it, shoes with spikes and has his own glove. The catcher has a special glove plus a mask, chest protector and shin guards.

__History of Jacks__

Jacks, as we know it today, is a game often played by children using ten metal objects with six points and a ball. The game probably came from "pebble Jacks," a game still played in Europe and Asia. A similar, and even older, game originated in Asia using the knucklebones of small animals.

__Chess Pieces__

Pieces used in chess are called: Pawn, Knight, Bishop, Rook, Queen and King. Rules govern their moves. The pieces, also called men, may be assigned different values according to their position and relation to other men during a game.

What do all these paragraphs have in common? __All about games or sports__

Page 100

Thinking Skills   Name _____

Guess What?

Look at each square. A part of something is showing. Write what you think it is below each square. __Answers will vary.__

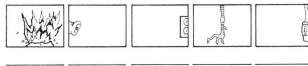

Answer Key

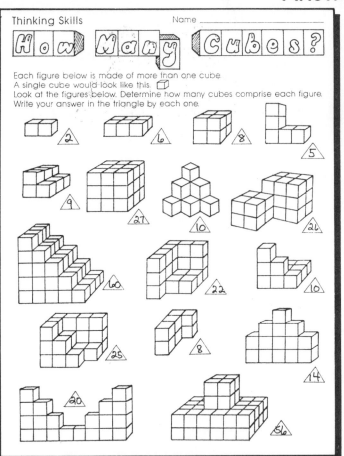

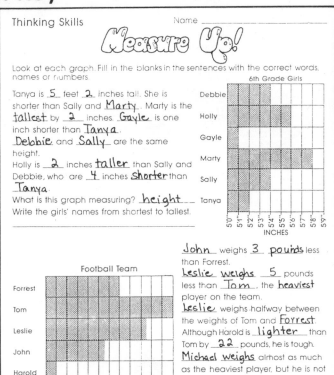

Page 101

Page 102

About the book . . .

If you're looking for one book that covers all the basic reading skills, you have just found it. They're all here: following directions, sequencing, vocabulary development, getting the main idea, drawing conclusions, etc., all presented in a highly creative manner which requires thinking on the part of your students.

We have made the activities highly independent in nature, plus provided you with an answer key, so that the time and effort these activities require will be your students', not yours.

About the author . . .

Holly Fitzgerald's special expertise in all areas of Language Arts has been gained by over fifteen years of varied teaching experiences at the elementary level. She holds a Master's Degree in Education from Vanderbilt University.

Author: Holly Fitzgerald
Editor: Lee Quackenbush
Artist/Production: Pat Biggs, Ann Stein
Production: Jan Daley, Mike Denhof
Cover Photo: Frank Pieroni
Art Consultant: Jan Vonk